easy peasy

laid-back food for lazy days

easy
peasy

laid-back food
for lazy days

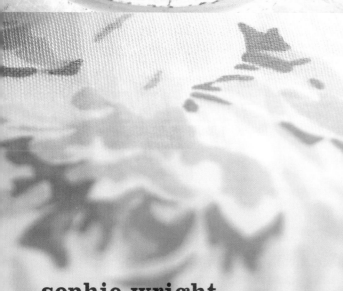

sophie wright

photography by kate whitaker

Kyle Cathie Ltd

*I would like to dedicate this book to everyone
who has taught and inspired me.*

First published in Great Britain in 2008 by
Kyle Cathie Limited
122 Arlington Road
London NW1 7HP
general.enquiries@kyle-cathie.com
www.kylecathie.com

ISBN 978 1 85626 787 8

Text © 2008 Sophie Wright
Design © 2008 Kyle Cathie Limited
Photographs © 2008 Kate Whitaker

Project editor Danielle Di Michiel
Photography by Kate Whitaker
Designed by Nicky Collings
Illustrations by Aaron Blecha
Home economy by Lizzie Harris
Styling by Wei Tang
Copyediting by Stephanie Evans
Production by Sha Huxtable

A Cataloguing in Publication record for this title is
available from the British Library.

Colour reproduction by Sang Choy
Printed in China by SNP Leefung

contents

the simple things in life

Easy peasy recipes are perfect for our chaotic lives. Sure, a complicated gastronomic feast based on twenty interesting and exotic ingredients will give you loads of personal satisfaction, but really, do you always have the time and energy?

I'm not going to scare you with ingredients or techniques you've never heard of, instead I'm going to show even the most inexperienced of cooks how cooking can become a part of everyday life. It's okay if things go wrong occasionally; how else will you ever learn?

I'm a firm believer that the simple things in life are often the best. Experiment with brunches and suppers over the weekend when you tend to have a little more time on your hands. Then you can get going on some simple, quick and satisfying ideas for your kids or for your own work lunchbox.

People tend to think that cooking is hard work but trust me, it isn't. It just takes common sense and a bit of preparation. I want you to think, 'I could do that' as you flip through these pages. Or, even better, 'I would really enjoy making that'. Change your ideas: don't associate cooking with being stuck in the kitchen. It should be about bringing family and friends together. Eating is sociable.

And, as you gain confidence, use this book as inspiration. If you don't like a particular ingredient, leave it out or replace it with something else. Don't be imprisoned by imaginary rules, but don't be frightened either. I'll still provide you with plenty of hints and tips to get you going.

Hopefully I can give you the confidence to cook something you wouldn't normally cook. Alongside the straightforward dishes, I hope you find a few things that will push your culinary boundaries.

Inside you will find a mixture of things, including influences from my travels and traditional grub handed down from my mum and nan. They will, I hope, give you the little boost you need to get into the kitchen on a Sunday morning and prepare that delicious brunch that will warm you for the rest of the day. Well... until lunchtime at least.

Keep it easy, open a bottle of wine and chill. Take your time and relax, that's what cooking should really be about.

Sophie x

bare essentials

You don't need to spend a fortune on equipment – concentrate on good-quality products and don't be swayed by gimmicks. Here are the things that every cook needs to make their life a little easier.

Chopping board

A good-quality wooden chopping board will look great in your kitchen and make your chopping chores a whole lot easier. A heavy board wont slip around as much as a lightweight plastic one. To reduce the risk of food poisoning, have a separate board for raw meat and fish.

Good-quality knives

A sharp knife is a safe knife. A blunt knife will damage your food and your fingers. Plus, your chopping will take twice as long. Do yourself a favour and pick up a couple of good-quality professional knives. You don't need to buy a whole set straight away, and don't forget to get the steel to sharpen your knives!

Baking trays and roasting tins

It's essential to have a small selection of these. It is worth spending a bit of money since they will last forever.

Utensils

Silicone cooking utensils will protect your non-stick pans from scratching. As a start, get your hands on a small and medium statula, a set of rubber-tipped tongs and a medium-sized whisk.

Speed peeler

Old-fashioned potato peelers should be banned! These can be used for anything from peeling your butternut squash to making cucumber ribbons.

Non-stick pan

Does exactly what it says on the tin; sticking fish skin will be a thing of the past.

Casserole dish with lid

A solid, heavy-based one is worth the investment. It will become your best friend and you won't know how you lived without it. A good one will last forever, so don't moan about spending a little more.

Microfine grater

The Gucci of graters. Fantastic for ginger, garlic, lemon and lime zest and equally fab for cheese. Nothing will get stuck inside and you won't spend half the time trying to extract bits of lemon zest from the tiny, knobbly bits of your grater.

Non-stick loaf tin

Many more uses than just making bread: think of terrines, layered ices, date and walnut loaf.

Non-stick flan case

Buy one with a removable base so not to crack the edges of your perfectly formed pastry case.

brunch

The best meal of the day. Brunch should not be restricted to those hours before noon – eat it when you like! Start your lazy weekend with one of these tasty ideas, whether it's a juicy sausage sandwich or just some muesli and fruit. 'Bigger is better' is my morning mantra. Finish it off with a fresh pot of coffee or some freshly-squeezed juice.

blueberry & banana pancakes

A wonderfully naughty-but-nice snack for the morning. It's sweet but goes fantastically well with savoury breakfast fare. We love pork and apple so why not bacon and eggs with banana? (That sorry old brown one sitting in the fruit bowl is fine, incidentally.) And, in case you were wondering, these indulgent delights go equally well with lashings of maple syrup and a splodge of crème fraîche.

MAKES 6–8

250g plain flour
2 teaspoons baking powder
Pinch of salt
1 tablespoon caster sugar
2 eggs
Drop of vanilla extract
1 ripe banana, mashed with a fork
About 300ml milk
A large handful of juicy blueberries
1 tablespoon vegetable oil
50g butter

1 Sift the flour, baking powder and the salt into a large mixing bowl and add the sugar. Make a well in the centre, crack in the eggs and add the vanilla. Using a whisk, slowly break up the eggs and start pulling in the flour from the sides. The slower you do this, the fewer lumps you'll have.

2 Add the mashed banana and start to add the milk a little at a time (you may need more or less, so keep whisking until you have the consistency you want). These are American-style pancakes and you want them to hold their shape in the pan so keep the batter on the thickish side. Lastly, throw in the blueberries, whole.

3 Now heat together the oil and butter in a large non-stick frying pan over a medium heat. You should manage about three 10cm pancakes in each batch. Don't overcrowd your pan or you'll end up with one large, unattractive mess.

4 Take a large spoonful of the mixture and push it off the spoon into the pan. This is easily done with the aid of another spoon. Try to make them as round as possible. The blueberries will burst when they hit the hot pan so don't be surprised.

5 Cook for about 2 minutes or until bubbles start to appear on the surface of the pancakes. Flip over the pancakes and cook for a further minute. When they are ready, they should be golden brown and slightly puffed up.

6 Continue to cook in batches until all the batter is used. Your cooked pancakes will keep warm on a plate covered with tin foil.

 TIP Quantities are just a guide when it comes to pancake and batter making. It's all about the consistency, because different flour varieties absorb different amounts of liquid. The batter is perfect when it drops slowly off the spoon, completely coating it. Watch out for lumps – give them a good whisk! And remember, a non-stick pan is essential for an easy life.

sweet gypsy toast

My Nan used to make her savoury version of this as an after-school snack to keep us quiet until dinner. We loved to dip ours into huge amounts of ketchup, but now I prefer a sweeter alternative. On this occasion – and this occasion only – I will say that pappy white bread is the only option. Personally, I can quite easily eat two slices of this without any problem, so I've made the recipe based on 4 people.

SERVES 4

FOR THE BLACKBERRY COULIS

120g blackberries
2 tablespoons icing sugar
1 tablespoon water

8 rashers streaky bacon
A handful of pecans

FOR THE TOAST

4 eggs, whisked
300ml milk
100g caster sugar
Pinch of salt
50g butter
1 tablespoon vegetable oil
8 slices white bread

1 For the coulis, whizz half the blackberries with the sugar. Taste and add a touch more sugar if it's not sweet enough for your liking. Add the water and pass through a tea strainer into a jug to remove the pips. Set aside.

2 For the toast, combine the whisked eggs with the milk, sugar and salt. Mix well. Heat a large non-stick frying pan with some of the butter and the oil over a medium heat. Dip a slice of the bread in the eggy mix. When the oil is hot enough, lay the bread in the pan away from you to avoid any hot oil splashing your hand. When the bread is golden brown on the underside, flip it over. Each slice will take about 2–3 minutes in total to cook. Don't overcrowd your pan – you can keep the cooked slices warm while you fry the rest.

3 Meanwhile, grill the bacon and lay a rasher on top of the golden brown eggy bread. Add a sprinkling of pecans, a drizzle of coulis and scatter with the remaining half of the berries.

TIP This can be made with any sad and lonely bread product that you may have lying around in your bread bin. Brioche and croissants are fantastic, but hot cross buns and even crumpets work well. Try making a jam sandwich and frying that – it's yum!

the healthy option

Muesli and fresh fruit will give you the best kick-start in the morning. You can make your own muesli and keep it in your cupboard for weeks, just as you would with a shop-bought variety. The major benefit of this is choosing exactly what you like to have in your own cereal. There's always something I don't like in the pre-mixed boxes – usually those horrible bits of cremated coconut you find at the bottom of the bag! One final thought: there is no wheat here, which is a bonus for people trying to reduce their intake.

500g oat flakes
500g barley flakes

WHATEVER YOU LIKE OF THE FOLLOWING DRIED FRUIT AND NUTS, SMALL HANDFULS:
Plump sultanas
Dried mango
Sunflower seeds
Flaked almonds
Pecans
Chopped dried apricots

1 Mix together the oat and barley flakes and your choice of dried fruit and nuts. Make up a big batch and keep it in a sealed container. When you fancy a bowl, top with your choice of fresh fruit.

PLUS WHATEVER YOU LIKE OF THE FOLLOWING OR YOUR OWN FAVOURITE FRUITS:
Fresh strawberries
Fresh raspberries
Fresh pear, sliced
Fresh kiwi
Fresh mango

2–3 tablespoons natural yogurt
Tiny splash of milk
Honey, for drizzling

Mix it all together well. Add the natural yogurt, a tiny splash of milk to moisten it a bit, and a drizzle of honey.

14 **TIP** As a delicious sweet alternative, make a Really Rich Chocolate Sauce (see page 157), mash in a banana and spread generously over the crêpe.

ricotta, basil and pinenut crêpe

Ricotta is a fab cheese to use in a dish like this as its flavour isn't overpowering. It does melt when heated, but unlike ordinary cheese it becomes more runny than gooey and creates a fantastic sauce.

SERVES 4

FOR THE CRÊPE
5 tablespoons flour
2 eggs
100ml milk
Salt and freshly ground black pepper

50g butter

FOR THE FILLING
100g toasted pinenuts
200g ricotta
Zest and juice of 1 lemon
A bunch of basil

1 Place the flour in a bowl and make a well in the centre. Break the eggs into the centre and use a whisk to start to combine the eggs with the flour. Start from the middle and slowly pull in the flour from around the outside of the bowl. This prevents any lumps from forming. Next, gradually start to add the milk, a little at a time, until all the milk has been added and you are left with a smooth batter. It should be the consistency of a runny yogurt. If it's a little thick, add a touch more milk. Season with salt and pepper.

2 To make the filling, toast the pinenuts in a dry frying pan until golden brown. Watch them carefully, as they can burn easily. Put the ricotta in a bowl and add the lemon zest and juice. Tear in the basil leaves and season with salt and pepper. Tip in the pinenuts and mix well.

3 Heat a large non-stick frying pan until nice and hot and add a small amount of the butter. Spoon in a ladleful of the batter, and quickly tilt the pan around to spread the mixture evenly. After about 30 seconds, check the bottom of the crêpe. If it is golden brown, turn it over in the pan. Immediately spread a generous spoonful of the ricotta mix evenly over the surface. Fold the crêpe in half then in half again to make a triangle. Serve.

raspberry & peach muffins

Muffins are a great way to start the day: moist and juicy, sticky and succulent. Not something you would bother to do everyday, I know, but great as a treat. They don't take as much time to prepare as you might think. Actually, they are very easy and will have your house smelling amazing!

MAKES 12 MUFFINS

2 eggs
100g granulated sugar
100g soft brown sugar
275ml milk
120ml vegetable oil

375g plain flour
4 teaspoons baking powder
Pinch of salt
120g raspberries
2 peaches, skinned, stoned and diced (or 4 halves
    of tinned peaches)

1 Place the eggs, sugars, milk and oil together in a large mixing bowl and whisk well until slightly fluffy – the fluffier the mix, the lighter your muffins.

2 Sift the flour, baking powder and salt into a separate bowl. Use a metal spoon to fold the flour mix carefully into the egg mixture, trying to keep as much air inside the mix as possible. Add the fruit.

3 Fill a 12-hole muffin tray with muffin papers and fill each one with the mix almost to the top. Place in the oven and cook for about 25 minutes. To check they are cooked all the way though, pierce one muffin with a knife. If it comes out clean, they're ready.

4 Leave to cool slightly if you can resist.

 TIP Avoid using the fan setting in your oven if possible as it will dry out your baking.

17

the unladylike sandwich

There is no possible way to eat this sandwich without getting it all over you so consume while you're still in your pyjamas! My general rule is that breakfast – or brunch – can be eaten at any time after 12am, especially at 3am after a night out. This feast is my ultimate favourite; the classics are always the best! I recommend keeping a stash of good sausages in the freezer for 3am emergencies.

SERVES 4

1 loaf sour dough bread, cut into 8 thick slices
3–4 tablespoons olive oil, plus extra for drizzling
2 large red onions, sliced
2 teaspoons sugar
Salt and freshly ground black pepper

2 tablespoons balsamic vinegar
8 good-quality sausages (your choice)
8 baby plum tomatoes, halved
1 tablespoon water
3 big handfuls of rocket
English mustard

1 Drizzle each slice of bread with a little olive oil, place on a griddle and toast lightly on both sides.

2 Heat 1 teaspoon of the oil in a pan, and add the onions. Allow them to sweat (that is, cook over a very low heat without colouring). When they start to wilt, add half the sugar, a pinch of salt, twist of pepper and half the balsamic vinegar. Cook for a further 3–4 minutes.

3 Now, start to cook the sausages in a frying pan in a tablespoon of the oil. When they are coloured on all sides, turn down the heat and cook for a further 6–8 minutes.

4 Now place the tomato halves in the pan with the onions. Add the water and the remaining sugar and balsamic, season again, and allow to reduce a little on a medium heat.

5 To assemble, cut the cooked sausages in half and lengthways. Spoon the tomato and onion mix over 4 slices of the bread, pop the sausages on top. Add a handful of rocket, drizzle with more oil, top with another slice of bread that has been smothered in mustard, plus extra to dip.

smoked salmon & scrambled eggs

on homemade english muffins with chive hollandaise

SERVES 4

FOR THE MUFFINS
6g dried yeast
½ teaspoon sugar
120ml warm milk (blood temperature)
225g plain flour
Pinch of salt
1 tablespoon vegetable oil, for frying

Hollandaise Sauce (see page 152)

Snipped chives
Squeeze of lemon

FOR THE SCRAMBLED EGGS
8 large free-range eggs
40g butter, cut into small cubes, plus a little extra
    for spreading
2 tablespoons extra-thick double cream
Salt and freshly ground black pepper
8 slices good-quality smoked salmon (it's worth
    investing in better quality)

1 First make the muffins. Dissolve the yeast and the sugar in a little of the milk. Don't add the salt yet.

2 Sift the flour into a large mixing bowl, add the salt and make a well in the centre. Pour the dissolved yeast mixture into the well and combine it all using your fingertips until it forms a dough-like texture. Cover the bowl with a tea towel and leave somewhere warm for 30 minutes or until the dough has doubled in size.

3 Dust your work surface with flour, remove the dough from the bowl and roll out to about 1cm thick. Cut into 8 rounds, each about 6–8cm in diameter.

4 Heat a non-stick pan with the oil and add the muffin rounds (work in batches, as necessary). Cook on a very low heat for 5–7 minutes on each side. They should be slightly golden brown.

5 Meanwhile, make the Hollandaise sauce, adding the chives and squeeze of lemon at the end. Set aside in a warm place.

6 For perfect scrambled eggs, break the eggs into a heavy-based pan and add half the cubed butter. Slowly stir with a spatula to incorporate the yolks with the whites until the eggs start to set. Keep moving the pan on and off the heat so that the eggs don't get too hot and turn rubbery.

7 When the eggs are the consistency you like – I like mine soft – add the cream and remaining butter. Adding them at the last minute not only adds richness but also stops the cooking process. Season with plenty of salt and pepper.

8 To serve, open up a slightly cooled muffin and lightly toast. Spread with a little butter then spoon on the eggs, followed by a slice of salmon and a generous dollop of Hollandaise.

TIP When preparing your eggs, never season before cooking. This starts the cooking process before you're ready and the eggs will start to break down, losing texture and flavour. Save your seasoning until the end.

soft-baked duck egg

with spinach, bacon, sauté mushrooms and marmite soldiers

Runny eggs are surely one of the best things in life! I love duck eggs because they are so much richer, and because they tend to have more yolk for soaking up with bread.

SERVES 4

50g butter, plus extra for greasing
Salt and freshly ground black pepper
4 rashers smoked streaky bacon, cut into cubes
400g baby spinach
4 duck eggs
6 chestnut mushrooms, sliced
1 garlic clove, grated

TO SERVE

Loaf of your favourite bread, toasted and
    cut into fingers
Butter, for spreading
Marmite, for spreading – love it or hate it!

1 For this you will need ramekins or smallish individual bowls. Grease the ramekins with butter and season them with salt and pepper. This will season the dish the whole way through.

2 Preheat the oven to 180°C/350°F/Gas Mark 4.

3 Heat a frying pan and fry the bacon on a high heat for a couple of minutes until the fat starts to bubble and the bacon bits turn crispy. Turn out of the pan onto kitchen paper.

4 Melt a knob of the butter in the bacon pan, add the spinach and allow to wilt. Season with plenty of salt and black pepper. When cooked and wilted, place on another sheet of kitchen paper, put a plate on top and push down so that the water is squeezed out.

5 Now lay the spinach in the bottom of each ramekin, topped by the bacon. Carefully crack one egg over the top of each ramekin and place in the oven for 4–5 minutes, depending on how runny you like your egg.

6 Meanwhile, melt the rest of the butter in a pan and sweat off your mushrooms. Add a twist of pepper and the garlic. Spoon over the top of the egg when cooked. Serve with toasted bread fingers smothered in butter and Marmite.

a french breakfast

… well not really

Surely hot ham and molten cheese must be one of the best ways of making the French croissant even yummier? There's nothing more satisfying than making something that is already one of life's luxuries even more wonderful and – being a savoury girl – I can't think of a better way to do it.

The classic way to make this dish takes time and patience. That's fine when you want to be in the cooking zone, but quite frankly, I often don't feel that way early in the day, so I've come up with a cheat's alternative. If French, please turn away now.

Normally you make a roux sauce – a combination of flour and butter bubbled together with milk added slowly. Instead I use mascarpone cheese and a little extra-thick double cream. A few more calories, but who cares?

SERVES 2

100g mascarpone
2 tablespoons extra-thick double cream
150g gruyère cheese, grated
Salt and freshly ground black pepper

1 egg yolk
25g butter
6 chestnut mushrooms, sliced
4 croissants
4 slices Parma or Serrano ham

1 Place the mascarpone and the double cream in a saucepan and bring to the boil. When the mixture boils, add half the gruyère cheese, season with salt and allow to cool. When cooled, add the egg yolk and mix well to help it to glaze when grilled.

2 Heat a frying pan and add the butter. When the butter starts to foam, add the mushrooms. When they have wilted, turn off the heat. Season with salt and pepper.

3 Slice open the croissants across the top and pour in a spoonful of the cream mix, followed by a slice of ham, a few sauté mushrooms, an extra drizzle of cream and then top it off with more cheese.

4 Grill until the cheese has melted and the cream has started to glaze. Eat immediately.

posh lunchbox

I'd love to encourage even the busiest of people to think about eating better. Not just in the evening, but also at lunch. So many of us have really bad eating habits when it comes to lunch. Mostly we fall victim to the coffee and carbs combination. Why not prepare yourself a tasty salad instead? Or perhaps you'd prefer to pick at a few healthy dips? Finish it off with a homemade granola bar rather than a sugar-full chocolate bar. Let's hope your healthy ways rub off on your less willing colleagues.

pear, pancetta, toasted pinenut & endive salad

All too often you make a yummy, healthy salad option only to find, come lunchtime, it's turned soggy and unappetising. This one's great – it's substantial and won't spoil easily. Red endive is a delicious ingredient: a cross between Belgian endive and radicchio de Treviso. Keep the dressing separate until you are ready to eat it – that way you're guaranteed a crispy salad.

SERVES 1 HUNGRY PERSON

1 unpeeled pear, cored
1 head red endive, end removed
A handful of pinenuts, toasted
100g smoked pancetta, diced
Half a handful of chervil, chopped
Fennel tops (fronds), chopped

FOR THE DRESSING

2 tablespoons sherry vinegar
1 tablespoon honey
1 teaspoon whole-grain mustard
3 tablespoons extra virgin olive oil
Pinch of salt

1 Cut the pear into 8 pieces. Don't be tempted to make the pieces smaller, otherwise they will bruise and taste horrible.

2 Peel the leaves apart on the endive and mix with the pear.

3 Toast the pinenuts in a dry frying pan. Remove them from the pan as soon as you can smell them toasting. Throw in the pancetta and allow to bubble and crisp for a few minutes. Remove, leave to cool and then add to the salad, along with the roughly chopped chervil and fennel fronds.

4 For the dressing, simply combine all the ingredients. Don't add too much salt because there's already a lot in the pancetta. Pour it into a jar.

5 Seal the dressing and salad separately, throw into your bag and try to resist until lunchtime.

lunchbox dips

Dips are great snacks or lunchbox fillers. There are heaps of varieties, showing influences from all over the world, but here's a small selection of my faves. If you're like me, you'll have trouble choosing between them! If you have any left over, these dips will keep in the fridge in an airtight container for up to three days.

roasted butternut squash & honey dip

The nice thing about squash is that it's so sweet you forget it's a healthy vegetable. Made into a dip, it is perfect with raw vegetables. It can also be served with dinner as a hot purée. Cooked well, butternut squash has a velvety butteryness that you can't get from other vegetables.

SERVES 4

2 small or 1 large butternut squash, peeled
2 sprigs of thyme
Pinch of Maldon sea salt

Freshly ground black pepper
½ teaspoon ground cumin
2–3 tablespoons honey
3 tablespoons olive oil

1 Preheat the oven to 180°C/350°F/Gas Mark 4.

2 The easiest way to peel your squash is with a speed peeler – no point wrestling with a knife if it can be avoided. Halve the squash lengthways and remove the seeds with a spoon. Cut the squash into 2.5cm chunks and place on a baking tray.

3 Strip the thyme leaves from the stalks and sprinkle them over the squash along with the salt, pepper and cumin. Drizzle over the honey followed by the oil. Ensure the squash is well coated by turning the pieces over in the tray. Roast for 20–30 minutes.

Keep your eye on it, and if the honey starts to caramelise, reduce the temperature slightly. However, a little singeing round the edges gives a nice deep flavour.

4 To check whether it's cooked, insert a knife into the squash. If there's no resistance, it's ready. Remove the tray from the oven and put the squash into a food-processor. Pulse until smooth but with some texture still remaining. If it seems too thick, add a little extra oil.

aubergine dip (baba ghanoush)

**SERVES 4 LITTLE PIGGIES
OR 6 PLEASANT PICKERS**

3–4 whole aubergines, depending on size
2 tablespoons olive oil
2 garlic cloves, crushed

Juice of 2 lemons
2 teaspoons tahini (sesame seed paste,
   found in most supermarkets)
½ teaspoon ground cumin
Salt and freshly ground pepper
Tiny pinch of cayenne

1 Preheat the oven to 180°C/350°F/Gas Mark 4.

2 Rub the aubergines with a little of the oil.
Place them on a baking tray and roast for about
35 minutes or until they have started to go all
wrinkly. Remove from the oven and allow them to
cool enough to handle. Cut them in half and use a
spoon to scrape all the squashy insides into a bowl.
Discard the skins.

3 Add all the remaining ingredients, mix together,
and season to taste with salt, black pepper and a
pinch of cayenne.

spicy cherry tomato salsa

SERVES 4

12–15 baby plum tomatoes, cut into quarters
1 red onion, chopped as finely as possible
2 tablespoons freshly chopped coriander
2 tablespoons finely chopped chives
3–4 tablespoons olive oil

Zest and juice of 2 limes
1 teaspoon caster sugar
1½ large red chillies, finely chopped, seeds left in
1 garlic clove, peeled and grated on a microfine grater
Pinch of Maldon sea salt
Freshly ground black pepper

1 Prepare all the ingredients and place everything in
a bowl. Taste and correct the seasoning.

 TIP Before making the Spicy Cherry Tomato Salsa, try roasting the tomatoes with a few red
peppers. Take the skins off before chopping and mixing with the rest of the ingredients.

homemade coleslaw & ham pitta

Homemade coleslaw is completely different from even the better-quality coleslaw you can buy. The supermarket variety is never fresh or crispy and way too overloaded with mayonnaise to be any good for kids or for yourself. I use crème fraîche; it's lighter and much better for you.

SERVES 6

FOR THE COLESLAW
½ white cabbage, sliced as thinly as possible
1 carrot, grated
1 celery stick, sliced thinly on the angle
A handful of raisins
1 apple, sliced thinly into strips

100g crème fraîche
1 lemon
Salt and freshly ground black pepper

TO SERVE
Packet of 6 pitta bread
2 handfuls homemade maple-glazed ham hock
   (see the recipe on page 97) or buy it hand-carved
   from the deli counter

1 Combine all of the prepared ingredients in a bowl, add the crème fraîche and lemon juice and season to taste.

2 To serve, open up the pitta bread, fill with as much of the tender flaky ham hock as you can, and add lashings of the lovely coleslaw.

feta, mint, broadbean & pea salad

This salad is colourful, quick, fresh and healthy – the perfect choice when you're making a lunch for the road. All you need is a container, no special equipment is required and it can be done in seconds.

SERVES 2

100g feta cheese
100g frozen peas
100g broad beans, fresh or frozen

½ bunch of mint
Juice of 1 lemon
50ml olive oil
Salt and freshly ground black pepper

1 Crumble the feta into a sealable container. Add the peas and broad beans. No need to remove the outer skin of the beans and don't worry if they're slightly frozen; they will be defrosted by the time you eat.

2 Tear the mint into the ingredients, add the lemon juice and the olive oil.

3 Season well. Place the lid on top and off you go!

griddled tuna

with new potatoes, black olives, capers, lemon & parsley

Everyone needs something to look forward to as they sit at their desk glaring at a PC. Here's the perfect fix – it's healthy, fresh, light and so tasty.

SERVES 2

100g baby new potatoes
2 teaspoons capers
2 tablespoons black olives, halved
Zest and juice of 1 lemon,
    plus juice of ½ lemon, to serve

50ml extra virgin olive oil, plus extra for drizzling
150g tuna loin
Maldon sea salt and freshly ground black pepper
1½ bunches of flat leaf parsley, chopped

1 Cook the new potatoes in boiling salted water until tender and drain.

2 Add the capers, olives, lemon zest, lemon juice from 1 lemon and olive oil to the warm potatoes and leave to marinate. If you have the time, this can be left covered in the fridge overnight, it will intensify the flavours.

3 Meanwhile, heat a griddle pan. Drizzle the tuna loin with oil and season with salt. When the pan is red hot, slap on the tuna and cook for 2 minutes then turn it over and cook for a further 2 minutes for a rare tuna steak. If you prefer it more cooked, leave it on the griddle for a further minute or so. When cooked, squeeze over the juice of half a lemon and remove from the griddle.

4 Stir the parsley into the potatoes and taste for seasoning. Slice the tuna in half and serve on top of the potatoes, drizzled with a little extra oil.

fresh berry smoothie

There is no definitive recipe for this smoothie. I would recommend going to the supermarket, buying whatever berries look a bit worst for wear and transforming them into something delicious. Alternatively, frozen berries are just as good, cheap and keep forever. They may need a bit more sugar to sweeten, though.

175ml apple juice
75g raspberries
6–8 strawberries
½ banana

Squeeze of lemon juice
2–3 teaspoons sugar
3–4 sprigs of fresh mint

1 Whizz everything in a blender or food-processor, pour into a sealable bottle and chill.

TIP   Any fruit that is ripe will blitz well in a smoothie. Pineapple works really well.

granola bars

These granola bars are great when you're on the go; I can't think of a better energy boost. They're full of all the right things that none of us get enough of! Treat this recipe as a guide – you can use whatever fruit and nuts you like as long as the quantities are roughly the same.

MAKES 16 BARS

Butter, for greasing
50g unsalted butter
200g runny honey
225g rolled oats
50g sunflower seeds

50g whole almonds
40g whole hazelnuts
200g dried fruit of your choice (figs, dates, raisins, apricots, cherries, blueberries, cranberries)
50g pumpkin seeds

1 Preheat the oven to 180°C/350°F/Gas Mark 4. Butter and line an ovenproof dish measuring 30 x 20cm.

2 Melt the butter and honey in a saucepan. Add in the remaining ingredients and mix together really well. Pour into the prepared dish and place in the oven for 20 minutes or until golden brown.

3 Remove from the oven and leave to cool before turning out of the tray. Cut into rustic rectangles. They will keep for a week in an airtight container.

gingerbread cupcakes

Who says gingerbread is just for kids?

MAKES 8–10 CUPCAKES

175g butter, softened
175g caster sugar
4 eggs
350g plain flour
2 teaspoons baking powder
½ teaspoon allspice
½ teaspoon ground ginger
½ teaspoon ground cinnamon
½ teaspoon ground nutmeg

Pinch of salt
100ml milk
Zest of 1 orange
1 drop vanilla extract

FOR THE TOPPING
150g butter, softened
100g icing sugar
Zest of 1 orange
Pinch of ground ginger
Candied orange peel (optional)

1 Preheat the oven to 160°C/325°F/Gas Mark 3.

2 Cream together the butter and sugar. When light and fluffy, gradually add the eggs, one by one. It's really important to keep the mix moving all the time as you add the eggs. The cake will look as though it has split but don't worry, that's normal.

3 Sift together all the dry ingredients, and carefully fold them into the mixture. Add the milk, orange zest and vanilla. Stir well. Fold the flour in gently.

4 When everything is combined, spoon a tablespoon of the mixture into individual cupcake cases. (It's best to sit these inside little cupcake tins or Yorkshire pudding tins to ensure they rise evenly and don't spill out the sides.) Bake for 12–15 minutes.

5 Remove from the oven and leave to cool while you make the butter icing.

6 Cream the softened butter and icing sugar with a wooden spoon until smooth. Add the orange zest spread over the top of the cooled cakes. Top each one with a pinch of ground ginger and some candied orange peel if you wish.

high tea

This is all about fun! Have you ever wanted to surprise
friends with some fancy treats? They should be fun to make
and fun to eat. Probably not something you're going to make
every day, but something to be savoured when you do. So,
get down to the supermarket and stock up on your
dry-store goods!

sandwiches

The centrepiece of any high tea. Little savoury classics bursting with surprisingly powerful flavour. Your friends will love these, especially if you can get your hands on a tiered cake stand (see pages 44–45).

piccalilli

Piccalilli is a real British classic; sweet and sour, soft and crunchy pickle that goes perfectly with any cold meat or lunchtime sandwich. There are some great varieties available in supermarkets, but I find they tend to be all sauce and not enough vegetable. I like to make my own version, adding exactly what I want.

This honestly is quick to cook. The only bit that may take time is preparing the vegetables but please don't get too hung up on making them perfect; this is a rustic homemade pickle!

MAKES 2–3 MEDIUM-SIZED JARS

YOU NEED ABOUT 900G OF VEG; THESE ARE MY SUGGESTIONS:

250g cauliflower florets, trimmed to about 1cm
250g frozen baby silver skinned onions, left whole
150g green beans, cut into 1cm tubes
100g peeled celeriac cut into 1cm cubes
150g unpeeled cucumber, halved, seeds removed by scooping them out with a spoon, cut into 1cm dice
150g Maldon sea salt
1 litre malt vinegar

FOR THE LIQUOR

1 teaspoon pickling spices (available at all supermarkets in the spice section)
2 teaspoons turmeric
2 teaspoons ground ginger
1½ tablespoons English mustard powder
2 teaspoons mustard seeds
300g demerara sugar
1½ tablespoon cornflour
500ml malt vinegar

1 Place all the prepared vegetables in a large bowl and cover with the salt and vinegar. Leave to marinate overnight. This brines the vegetables, helping to flavour, season and preserve them.

2 The next day, thoroughly rinse the brine out of the vegetables and leave to drain.

3 To make the liquor, combine all the spices, mustards, sugar and cornflour together in a saucepan. Add a splash of the vinegar to make a paste. Add the remaining vinegar once the paste is smooth and bring to the boil over a low heat. Add the vegetables, cook for around 10–15 minutes, turn off the heat and leave to cool.

4 Decant into a clean and sterilised sealable jar. Piccalilli will keep for about three months in the fridge. To serve, spread over some crusty bread, slap on a few slices of maple-glazed ham hock (see page 97) and enjoy.

peppered crusted beef

To make this sandwich, you need a piece of roasted beef, probably left from dinner the night before.

MAKES 6–8 SANDWICHES

FOR THE PESTO
2 large bunches of fresh watercress
3cm knob of fresh horseradish, grated
50ml olive oil
Juice of ½ a lemon
1 garlic clove
Maldon sea salt and freshly ground black pepper

Piece of roasted beef, preferably topside
50g black peppercorns, crushed in a pestle and mortar
1 loaf of good-quality wholegrain bread, sliced

1 To make a pesto, tear the top leaves from the watercress and place in a blender with the horseradish, oil, lemon, garlic and seasoning. Whizz to a coarse paste. Add a little more oil if need be.

2 Next take the beef, and rub it with a small amount of olive oil then roll it in the crushed peppercorns and slice thinly.

3 Slice the bread as you like it and spread with a generous amount of your pesto then top with beef. Season with a little sea salt and a drizzle of oil.

smoked salmon & cucumber

This is surprisingly easy to make and tastes fabulous with cucumber on brown bread sandwiches, crusts off, of course! It's also great on toast or even folded through some tagliatelle for a quick supper. Smoked salmon trimmings are half the price of sliced salmon – take a look in your supermarket next time.

SERVES 6

FOR THE PÂTÉ
300g smoked salmon trimmings
Juice of 1 lemon
Salt and plenty of freshly ground black pepper
175g Philadelphia cheese
½ bunch of dill, leafy fronds only, chopped

½ cucumber
Butter, for spreading
Sliced brown bread, crusts removed

1 Place all the ingredients for the pâté in a food processor and whizz until smooth. Check for seasoning, add a little salt if necessary. Refrigerate until needed.

2 Build your sandwich by peeling and thinly slicing the cucumber. Butter the bread on both sides and spread with a generous helping of the pâté. Lay on the cucumber, overlapping the slices. Serve classically cut into fingers.

 **TIP** The smoked salmon pâté shouldn't be kept for longer than two days in the fridge.

  TIP You will know when your quiche is ready when it has a slight wobble. It will firm as it cools.

pink seafood quiche

One for the girls. Quiche is great hot or cold, as a light nibble or for dinner with a nice big salad. It might not be something you would make every day, but it will make a fantastic treat and is a great idea when entertaining.

MAKES A 22CM QUICHE/SERVES 8

Butter, for greasing
1 x Shortcrust Pastry recipe (see page 156)
Flour, for rolling

FOR THE POACHING LIQUOR
½ onion, peeled and roughly sliced
½ fennel bulb, roughly sliced
1 litre cold water
1 bay leaf
2 peppercorns
200ml white wine

FOR THE FILLING
300g salmon, preferably in one piece
100g crayfish (fresh is best but in brine is fine)
Zest of 1 lemon
2 teaspoons chopped dill

FOR THE EGG CUSTARD MIX
2 eggs
1 yolk
250ml double cream
50g grated Parmesan cheese
½ teaspoon cayenne pepper

1 Grease a 22cm flan case, preferably with a removable base.

2 First make the pastry and put in the fridge to rest for 30 minutes.

3 Remove from the fridge and place on a lightly floured surface. Roll out the pastry to about 2–3mm thick, roll onto the rolling pin and lay into the flan case. Gently ease the pastry to the corners. Trim the edges with a knife, prick the base and allow to rest for a further 15 minutes in the fridge.

4 Preheat the oven to 180°C/350°F/Gas Mark 4.

5 Line the pastry case with parchment and baking beans and bake for 10 minutes, then remove the beans and bake for a further 5 minutes.

6 Prepare the poaching liquor by putting all the ingredients in a shallow pan.

7 To make the filling, place the salmon in the pan, bring to the boil then turn off the heat and allow to cool. When completely cold, remove the salmon and gently flake it into the flan case, discarding the skin. Scatter the crayfish, lemon zest and dill on top.

8 For the egg custard, whisk together all the ingredients. Slowly pour the mixture into the case, filling the gaps between the fish, and bake at 170°C/325°F/Gas Mark 3 for 30–40 minutes or until the egg custard is firm when you gently shake the dish. Leave to cool before removing from the flan case.

9 Reheat gently if you want to serve it warm.

pork pâté

You may wonder why you'd bother to make pâté yourself when you can so easily buy it. Well, first you will know exactly what has gone into it and second you can adapt it to suit your taste. It really isn't hard to make, and it keeps in the fridge for up to a week so long as you clingfilm it properly.

You will need either a terrine mould or something that resembles one, such as a 500g loaf tin. Ideal with the homemade Apple Chutney on the opposite page.

MAKES 10–12 SLICES

Oil, for greasing
20 rashers streaky bacon
300g minced pork belly
300g minced pork liver
1 garlic clove, finely chopped
6 shallots, finely chopped
75g breadcrumbs
4 eggs, beaten

200g unsalted butter, melted
25ml Port
Leaves stripped from 2 sprigs of thyme
A handful of chopped parsley
½ teaspoon ground nutmeg
75ml double cream
1½ teaspoons salt
Lots of freshly ground black pepper

1 Preheat the oven to 130ºC/275°F/Gas Mark 1. Grease the mould with a little oil.

2 Stretch out a length of clingfilm longer than your mould then place another two layers on top of that. Smooth it out with your hand and then lay it into the mould, ensuring there are no air bubbles and that the clingfilm is tucked into all the corners.

3 Use the bacon to line the sides and the base of the mould, overlapping the rashers slightly, and leaving some hanging over the edges to cover the pâté later.

4 Next combine all the remaining ingredients together in a large mixing bowl. Make sure the egg is properly incorporated. Carefully pack the mixture into the terrine mould and fold the overhanging bacon across the top. Press down gently and cover the top tightly with tinfoil.

5 Place the terrine in a shallow tray and fill it halfway with boiling water (cooking it like this, in what is called a bain-marie, or water bath, keeps the terrine moist). Cook in the oven for 2 hours and 15 minutes, topping up the tray with more boiling water if necessary.

6 Take the tray from the oven, remove the terrine from its water bath and allow to cool. The terrine needs to be pressed. I cut a piece of cardboard to fit, place it on top and weigh it down with a couple of tins.

7 Leave the weighted terrine overnight in the fridge and turn it out the following day. Perfect for a picnic, served with some nice fresh bread and a big salad. Don't forget that chutney!

apple chutney

What could be better than a lovely fruity chutney to liven up a piece of cheese or pâté? In fact, it can be devilishly addictive.

MAKES 2–3 MEDIUM JARS

5 shallots, finely chopped
50g butter
750g firm apples, such as Cox or Granny Smith, peeled
250g pears, preferably Williams, peeled
1 cinnamon stick
2 cloves

½ teaspoon ground ginger
Zest and juice of 1 orange
150ml red wine vinegar
300g brown sugar
A handful of raisins
3 x 50ml water, to sterilise the jars

1 Sweat the shallots in the butter in a large pan until they are translucent. Add the apples and pears and turn up the heat. Keep stirring so that it doesn't burn. Add all the spices and the orange zest and juice. Mix well. Add the vinegar and the sugar. Put a lid on the pan, turn the heat right down to low and allow to stew.

2 After 20 minutes, add the raisins and continue to cook for up to an hour or until the chutney has thickened. Taste and adjust its sweetness or sharpness with a little more sugar or vinegar, but do remember that the flavours will become stronger as the chutney matures. Allow to cool.

3 Meanwhile, microwave your jars with 50ml water in the bottom of them to sterilise and remove any bacteria. Use the highest setting and microwave for 2 minutes. Wash the lids. The can also be boiled or put in the dishwasher.

4 Pour the cooled chutney into the jars and cover with clingfilm. Screw on the lid, label and, ideally, leave it alone for a week for the flavours to develop. This keeps for up to 6 months if the jars are properly sterilised.

TIP If the chutney looks too runny after all the fruit had cooked down, strain through a sieve and boil the liquor until it has reduced by about half, then add the fruit back into the reduced liquor and leave to cool.

duck with plum sauce pancakes

SERVES 6–8

FOR THE SEASONING

100g salt
1 teaspoon Chinese five-spice powder
1 teaspoon dried chilli
1 teaspoon ground cinnamon

FOR THE CRISPY DUCK

4 duck legs
1 cinnamon stick
5 peppercorns
2 bay leaves
Zest of 1 orange
400ml goose or duck fat
Sea salt flakes

FOR THE PLUM SAUCE

1 teaspoon vegetable oil
1 shallot, peeled and chopped
1 medium red chilli, chopped
400g ripe stoned plums, chopped finely
400g demerara sugar
300ml red wine vinegar
1 star anise
½ teaspoon Chinese five-spice

1 packet of Chinese pancakes (available from good
   supermarkets in the Oriental section)
6 spring onions, sliced on the angle
½ cucumber, peeled, deseeded and cut into strips

1 Mix together the ingredients for the seasoning. Score the fat on the duck legs and rub it with the salt-spice mix. Leave the legs in the fridge overnight in a non-metallic dish to inject loads of flavour.

2 When you're ready to cook, brush the salt-spice mix off the duck and give it a quick rinse under the tap.

3 Preheat the oven to 150°C/300°F/Gas Mark 2. Place the duck legs in a deep-sided baking tray, add in the spices and flavourings and pour over the goose fat. Put in the oven for 2 minutes.

4 Very carefully remove the legs from the fat and place on a wire rack. You might want to leave them to cool a bit first. The fat is no longer needed. Turn up the oven to 220°C/425°F/Gas Mark 7.

5 Season with the sea salt and return it to the oven. Place on the wire rack for 25 minutes to crisp the skin

slightly. Remove from the oven, shred the meat from the bone and set aside while you make the plum sauce.

6 Heat the oil in a pan and sweat off the shallots and chilli. When they have started to soften, add in the plums and allow to heat through. Start to cook down slightly. Add in the sugar, vinegar and the two spices. Allow the sauce to cook down on a low heat until pulpy and thick. The sweetness may need adjusting slightly depending on the ripeness of the plums.

7 Spread 1 teaspoon of the plum sauce over the base of a pancake. Add a small amount of shredded duck, sliced onions and 4 or 5 cucumber strips. Roll the pancake into a cigar shape. Make as many of these as you can with the mixture.

8 Serve with a little of the plum sauce.

fondant fancies

These are so cute and there are endless ways of decorating them. You could pick a few flowers or rose petals from the garden, or you can always buy fancy things to strew on top or decorate with chocolate piping. When preparing the icing, just add a drop of whatever food colouring you want. Lilac looks great.

MAKES 12

Butter, for greasing

FOR THE SPONGE
100g soft butter
100g caster sugar
2 eggs
Few drops of vanilla extract
100g plain flour, sifted

1 teaspoon baking powder
Jam, lemon curd or whipped cream, to fill (optional)

FOR THE ICING
500g fondant icing sugar, sifted
Juice of 1 lemon
A drop of food colouring, any shade you fancy

Decorations according to your whim

1 Preheat the oven to 180°C/350°F/Gas Mark 4. Butter and line a cake tin measuring about 25 x 20cm with baking parchment or use 2 loaf tins.

2 Cream together the butter and the sugar until well combined. Now add the eggs and the vanilla extract. The mix may look as if it is about to split. If this happens, add a small amount of the flour and gently fold into the mix.

3 Sift the flour with the baking powder several times to ensure the flour is well aerated – this is key to the nice light sponge you require. Fold in the dry ingredients with a metal spoon, pour into the prepared cake tin and bake for 25–30 minutes. Turn out of the tin and leave to cool.

4 Once cooled, turn the cake out and cut into 5 x 5cm squares. If you wish, cut the squares in half and sandwich with a layer of jam, lemon curd or fresh whipped cream.

5 To make the icing, combine the icing sugar with enough lemon juice to make a fondant that coats the back of a spoon. Add in the food colouring.

6 Place the fancies on a wire rack on a clean surface. It gets a little messy here but it's also great fun. Use a dessertspoon to pour a generous helping of icing directly over the top of each fancy. Leave to set. If your work looks a bit patchy, do a second coat once dry. Decorate with pretty things while still wet.

TIP To turn these into chocolaty fancies, just add 1 teaspoon of cocoa powder to the sponge mix. For chocolate icing, boil 250ml double cream, pour over 250g plain chocolate, broken into pieces. Stir until melted and combined, leave to cool slightly then pour over each fancy.

easy chocolate fudge

Who doesn't love fudge? All creamy and crumbly and delicious. You can make it in so many wonderful flavours. Here's a chocolate version. While this is fairly easy to prepare, sometimes it's not so easy to clean your saucepan afterwards. Squeeze a little washing liquid into it, add some water and put on the heat for a few moments. This should dislodge any stubborn bits.

MAKES 16–20 SQUARES

Butter, for greasing
125ml whole milk
450g sugar
1 tablespoon cocoa powder

25g butter
Few drops of vanilla
Sugar flowers, silver balls or chocolate buttons,
   to decorate

1 Grease and line a baking tray about 20cm square with sides at least 3cm deep. Line the sides and the base with baking parchment – no need for neatness.

2 Put the milk, sugar, cocoa, butter and vanilla in a pan and cook on a low heat. After a few minutes, when the mixture is starting to bubble slightly around the edges, use a spoon to drop a pea-sized piece of the fudge into a bowl of cold water. If the pea stays in a ball and you can pick it up and squeeze it between your fingers, it's ready. This is known as the 'soft ball' stage.

3 Remove from the heat and pour the fudge into the tray. Let it stand for a few minutes then add your decorations while the fudge is still hot so that they hold fast.

4 Leave to cool completely in the fridge before cutting into cubes and serving to very special friends!

red chilli chocolate brownies

The rule when cooking brownies is to be brave. The trick is to take them out of the oven before you actually think they're ready. It is essential that they are hot and squidgy in the middle. The red chillies may seem a bit of a strange ingredient, but chilli and chocolate is a really classic combo in many countries, especially Mexico. The chilli should cut through the richness of the chocolate, which is the reason for using a really good-quality chocolate here.

MAKES 16–18 SQUARES

Butter, for greasing
300g good-quality dark chocolate (70% cocoa solids),
    broken into pieces
250g hard butter, cut into cubes

5 eggs
325g caster sugar
200g plain flour
2 medium red chillies, deseeded and
    cut into thin strips
120g plain chocolate chips

1 Preheat the oven to 180°C/350°F/Gas Mark 4. As with most baking, try to avoid using the fan setting. Line the base and sides of a baking dish roughly 30 x 20cm and 4–5cm deep with buttered baking parchment.

2 Melt the chocolate and butter in a heatproof bowl over a pan of simmering water. Ensure the base of the bowl is not in contact with the water because if the chocolate gets too hot it will 'split'.

3 When everything has melted, remove the bowl from the heat and allow to cool. Beat together the eggs and the sugar and slowly pour the cooled melted chocolate mixture on top. Combine well.

4 Sift the flour and gently fold into the mixture. Now add the chillies and the chocolate chips. Pour into your prepared baking tin and bake for about 20–25 minutes or until the brownie looks cracked on top but still slightly undercooked. Don't forget, as it cools, the chocolate will start to set and the brownies will firm up.

hokey pokey pieces

A sticky, chewy piece of heaven is exactly what a Hokey Pokey piece is. A cross between the inside of a Crunchy Bar and a Worther's Original, I wouldn't recommend eating it every day unless you like going to the dentist, but it's certainly something for special occasions.

MAKES 25–30 SQUARES

5 tablespoons caster sugar
3 tablespoons golden syrup
1½ teaspoons baking powder

1 Grease and line a loaf tin with baking parchment. Place the tin in the freezer to get it nice and chilled.

2 Put the sugar and the golden syrup in a saucepan and slowly bring to the boil, stirring occasionally. Keep over the heat until the sugar starts to turn a golden brown then remove from the heat and whisk in the baking powder.

3 Immediately pour the mix into the chilled loaf tin and put in the fridge to set.

4 When the mix is hard, remove from the tin and smash into bite-sized pieces. Store them out of the fridge.

pink magic moments

I had no idea what to call these little gems. They're pink, very sweet, soft and sticky. Sounds like a magic moment to me! Once again the trusty – sometimes rusty – baking tray has to come out. And once again grease and line it. I'm sure you're good at that by now.

MAKES 30

Butter, for greasing
550g icing sugar
100ml milk
25g butter
Pinch of salt
125g desiccated coconut
Red food colouring

1 Grease and line a baking tin measuring about 25 x 20cm.

2 Put the icing sugar, milk, butter and salt in a pan and boil until it reaches the soft ball stage (see step 2, page 52). Add the coconut and mix through. Pour into another bowl and beat in the food colouring until the mixture starts to thicken. I like mine to be a fluorescent pink but the strength of the colour is entirely up to you!

3 Now pour the mix into the lined baking tray and leave to cool. Turn out and cut into squares to serve with a nice cup of tea.

TIP Hokey Pokey Pieces are also great smashed up into tiny pieces and folded through ice cream or sprinkled over a dessert.

general jam-making tips

Jam-making is all about how sweet your tooth is. If you're like me and like it less sweet, reduce the amount of sugar and allow the natural sweetness of the fruit to come through. Of course this depends on what jam you intend to make; strawberry jam will always be sweeter than raspberry jam, simply because strawberries are sweeter. Taste the jam throughout the process and judge for yourself (do take care: the jam is literally boiling hot).

Don't forget that you can always add but you can't take away, so go easy with sugar at first. Also, you don't want the fruit to be too ripe when making jam, as long as you like the bits, that is. If you don't like bits, your fruit needs to be ripe. Basically, you'll need equal amounts of fruit to sugar for quite a sweet jam. I always use a ratio of 3 parts sugar to 4 parts fruit.

Finally, do use jam or preserving sugar, which contains pectin. Pectin is what causes the jam to set; it is found naturally in most fruit, especially in citrus fruit and sharp-tasting ones such as apples, rhubarb, blackcurrants and raspberries.

rhubarb & ginger jam

You need jars with tight-fitting lids. Sterilise them by placing 50ml water in the bottom of each jar, without the lids, and microwave them on high for a couple of minutes. Run the lids through the dishwasher.

MAKES 4–5 SMALL JARS

2 x 10g knobs of butter
1.5kg rhubarb, cut into 2–3cm pieces

200g fresh ginger, peeled and sliced very thinly
  into strips
Zest of 1 lemon and juice of 2 lemons
1.25kg jam sugar (with pectin)

1 Before you start, place four small plates in the freezer. Rub the base of your preserving pan or your biggest, heaviest saucepan with a knob of butter.

2 Wash the rhubarb. Drain and dry well and place in your buttered pan. Add the ginger and the lemon zest. Sprinkle on the sugar. This is best left overnight covered, out of the fridge, to allow the sugar to slowly dissolve.

3 The next day, place the pan on a very low heat and allow the fruit to start to bleed into the sugar. Don't stir the pan at all. It won't burn provided the heat is low enough. Shake the pan when the juices have started to run a little and the sugar has dissolved. This should take about 10–12 minutes.

4 Now add the lemon juice, which will create steam. Turn up the heat and allow the jam to come to the boil. Boil for about 10 minutes. Turn down the heat.

5 Remove a small spoonful and place on one of your cold plates. Allow to cool and if it sets with a little skin, the jam is ready. If it doesn't, re-boil the jam and do the test again. Keep testing until it forms a skin on top.

6 Now stir in the second knob of butter and allow to cool slightly before pouring it into your sterilised jars, placing a jam paper on top, sealing tightly with the lid, and labelling.

strawberry or raspberry jam

Follow exactly the same process as the rhubarb, but substitute the rhubarb and ginger with 1.5kg strawberries or raspberries. If you don't want any bits, pass through a sieve once cooked. Be careful though, because the jam will be boiling hot.

  TIP Never put cooked pastry in the fridge if you can help it. The pastry will go soggy.

jam tarts

When I was a kid, I remember making these jam tarts every Sunday morning with my Mum. They're a fantastic way to get the kids involved, but just as satisfying to knock up on your own!

Making your own pastry becomes easier with practice, and it's worth it. I make these tarts with shortcrust pastry because once the jam is added, you're in for a sugar overload.

You will need some form of pastry cutter for this. You can use a bowl to cut round but that's far too much hard work if you ask me. A fluted edge pastry cutter about 8cm in diameter should do, and a little cutter, any shape you like, for the top. A star is nice or just a smaller version of what you originally used. You will also need a muffin tin or a 12-hole Yorkshire pudding pan.

MAKES 12 TARTS

1 x Shortcrust Pastry recipe (see page 156)
Homemade jam (see page 57)
Icing sugar, for dusting (optional)

1 First make the pastry and put in the fridge to rest for 30 minutes.

2 Preheat the oven to 180°C/350°F/Gas Mark 4. Grease and flour your tin.

3 Remove the pastry from the fridge and place on a lightly floured surface. Roll out the pastry to a thickness of about 2mm and cut out 12 rounds with the fluted cutter. Place each one into the prepared tin. Cut out 12 tops with your chosen cutter.

4 Spoon 1–1½ teaspoons of your homemade jam into each tart. It's nice to do a mixture of flavours. Place the lids on top and bake in the oven for about 12 minutes or until the tops are golden brown.

5 Once cooled slightly, remove from the tins, dust with icing sugar if you like and leave to cool completely. These will keep in an airtight container for 3–4 days.

date, fig & walnut loaf

All Mums love this one! It sounds sophisticated, it's a little spicy, but it's mega-easy to prepare.

MAKES 10–12 SLICES

120g softened butter, plus extra for greasing
180g dark soft brown sugar (muscovado is perfect)
3 eggs
225g plain flour
Pinch of salt
1½ teaspoons baking powder

100ml milk
100g dates, stone removed and roughly chopped
75g chopped figs
150g chopped walnuts
½ teaspoon ground ginger
½ teaspoon ground cinnamon
½ teaspoon ground cloves

1 Dig out your 20 x 8cm loaf tin and grease it with butter on all sides and the bottom.

2 Preheat the oven to 180ºC/350°F/Gas Mark 4, not on fan setting. If you can't turn your fan off, place an ovenproof bowl of water in the bottom of the oven to stop the loaf drying out.

3 Whisk together the butter and sugar, then slowly add the eggs. Sift in the flour, salt and baking powder and continue to whisk. Add the milk then fold in the dried fruit, nuts and spices. If it's still looking a tad dry, add another splash of milk.

4 Spoon into the loaf tin and even out the top with a spatula.

5 Place in the oven for about 45 minutes. When cooked, the cake should be a little bit sticky. Turn out of the tin and leave to cool on a wire rack.

6 Smother a slice with butter if you like. This would be great with a cup of real Earl Grey tea, served with lemon, not milk, of course!

summer specials

Summer is all about fresh, zingy flavours. Summer ingredients speak for themselves, they need very little attention to make them even more fantastic than they are, often just a squeeze of lemon or a splash of oil. This is sociable food; food that should be accompanied with a big glass of wine or ice-cold beer.

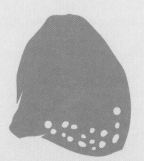

raspberry & lime ice tea

Homemade ice tea is nothing like the ice tea you would buy in a bottle. It's fresh, healthy and thirst-quenching. I like mine with raspberries, not just for the colour but also for the sharpness. Heaven on a hot day!

MAKES 6 GLASSES

200g raspberries, 6 whole ones reserved for decoration
100–120g caster sugar, depending on how sweet
   you like it
½ teaspoon bicarbonate of soda
Zest and juice of 2 limes, reserving 2 slices for decoration
500ml boiling water
2 black tea bags
500ml cold water

TO SERVE
Ice
Slices of lime
Berries, for decoration

1 Push the raspberries through a sieve using the back of a spoon and discard the seeds. Add the sugar and the bicarbonate of soda to the raspberry purée, then the zest and juice of the limes.

2 Pour the 500ml of boiling water onto the tea bags and allow to infuse for 2–3 minutes – no longer or the tea will start to go bitter. Remove the bags and allow to cool.

3 When cooled, pour on 500ml cold water and add the purée. Stir together in a big jug and taste for sweetness. Add a little more sugar if required. Serve over ice with a slice of lime and decorated with berries.

real lemonade

There's no substitute for real lemonade. It's one of the easiest things in the world to make but no one does it! Also, it probably costs less to make than to buy from the supermarket. This actually tastes of lemons unlike the sugary syrup that everyone thinks is lemonade.

MAKES 6 GLASSES

Zest and juice of 6 whole lemons, or more if you prefer
150g sugar
1.2 litres cold water

Mint leaves (optional), to serve

1 Put the lemon zest and juice in a jug. Add the sugar and mix until dissolved. Taste and add more lemons if you prefer it slightly zingier.

2 Pour on the water and place in the fridge, to allow the drink to infuse and chill thoroughly.

3 Serve over ice, and it's great with fresh mint.

 TIP If you prefer fizzy lemonade, use carbonated water.

chilled cucumber & almond soup

This is a great refreshing soup. Perfect for dinner parties, since it's served chilled, which means you can concentrate on preparing other things. It will keep well in the fridge for two days, or you can freeze it.

SERVES 4

150g ground almonds
2 slices stale white bread, crusts removed and soaked
   in 500ml ice water
3 cucumbers, peeled, halved lengthways, seeds
   removed with a spoon
1 garlic clove, crushed or grated
2 tablespoons crème fraîche

Juice of 1 lemon
Salt and freshly ground black pepper

TO GARNISH
Good-quality extra virgin olive oil
Flaked almonds, toasted

Sourdough bread, toasted, to serve

1 Put the ground almonds in a food-processor. Add the sliced soaked bread and pulse, reserving the soaking water.

2 Roughly chop the cucumber and add to the food-processor with the garlic. Whizz until smooth. Now add the crème fraîche and the reserved water. Add lemon juice to taste and plenty of salt and black pepper. Chill until needed.

3 Drizzle the extra virgin olive oil over and garnish with toasted flaked almonds. Serve with toasted sourdough bread.

seriously sexy
baked chilli pineapple

I wish I could take credit for this fabulous dish but unfortunately I can't. I first came across it in New Zealand and haven't looked back since. There is something very special about the spice of the chilli combined with the soothing sweetness of the pineapple. You really have to try it.

SERVES 4

1 super sweet pineapple
300g caster sugar
Seeds scraped from 1 vanilla pod
3 fresh red chillies, chopped

5cm knob of fresh ginger, peeled and grated
  on a microfine grater
100ml dark rum
1 tablespoon honey

1 Remove the skin from the pineapple and cut into 1cm thick rings. Remove the middle core.

2 Place the sugar, vanilla seeds, chillies and ginger in a pestle and mortar or a mini food-processor and whizz until fine. Mix in the rum and honey. Lay the pineapple slices on a tray and pour over the mixture. Leave to marinate for as long as you wish.

3 When you're ready to serve, preheat the oven to 200°C/400°F/Gas Mark 6. Cook the pineapple for 10–15 minutes – just long enough for it to heat through and for the sugars to start caramelising.

4 Remove from the oven and transfer to a serving plate with all the hot and spicy juices. Great with ice cream.

chilli crab cakes

with homemade lime mayo

Lime, chilli and crab: born to be together!

MAKES 12 SMALL CRAB CAKES

FOR THE LIME MAYONNAISE
2 egg yolks at room temperature
Zest of 2 limes and juice of 1 lime, to taste
1 teaspoon Dijon mustard
Pinch of sugar
Pinch of salt
½ garlic clove, crushed
250ml vegetable oil in a jug

FOR THE CRAB CAKES
2 red chillies, seeds removed, finely chopped
Zest and juice of 2 limes
Zest of 1 lemon
1 garlic clove, grated
A small bunch of coriander, leaves picked off and
    finely chopped
Large pinch of salt
450g white crabmeat, picked and checked for shell
100g brown crabmeat, picked and checked for shell
1 tablespoon Mayo (see page 153)
About 50g dried breadcrumbs (Japanese breadcrumbs,
    sold as panko, if you can get them)
Salt and freshly ground black pepper

FOR THE CRISPY COATING
2 eggs, beaten
100g flour
100g breadcrumbs (panko are best but fine
    breadcrumbs, bought or homemade, are okay)

1 For the lime mayonnaise, place the egg yolks in a bowl with the lime zest, mustard, sugar, salt and garlic. Mix thoroughly. Add the oil, drop by drop, whisking by hand until it is all mixed in. Add the lime juice to taste.

2 Next, make the crab cakes. Pound the finely chopped chilli, lime and lemon zest, garlic and coriander in a pestle and mortar with the salt. The salt acts as an abrasive and helps to form a smooth paste, ensuring an even distribution of flavour.

3 Mix the paste with the picked crabmeat. Mix it until the crab starts to take on a slight pinkish colour from the chillies. Add the lime juice and mayo and combine. Next add the breadcrumbs – just enough to make the mix mouldable – the amount depends on how wet your crabmeat is. Season.

4 Divide the mixture into 12 balls, each about 40–50g. Place in the fridge for 20 minutes.

5 For the coating, put the eggs, flour and breadcrumbs in separate bowls. Dip the mixture balls, one at a time, first into the flour, then the egg and finally the breadcrumbs, covering well. By hand, form little patty shapes about 2.5cm tall and dunk again into the egg and breadcrumbs. (This is called a double pane and gives the cakes a crispy coating, ensuring they don't burst open while cooking.)

6 Keep in the fridge until you are ready to prepare them. Since the crab is already cooked the cakes just need to be heated through. Either deep-fry at 180ºC or shallow-fry until golden brown in vegetable oil that is about 1cm deep. Dry on kitchen paper before serving with the lime mayonnaise.

baby squid

marinated in lime, green chilli & coriander

The ideal accompaniment to a hot summer's day. Great with a big green salad and a large glass of chilled white wine. People always think squid is scary to prepare, but once you've done it, it's actually quite easy the next time.

SERVES 4

FOR THE MARINADE

3 fresh green chillies, deseeded
A bunch of coriander, chopped, stalks included
2 garlic cloves
Zest and juice of 2 limes
½ stick of lemongrass, chopped
2–3 tablespoons olive oil
Pinch of salt

FOR THE SQUID

3 baby squid per person as a starter or light lunch
  or 1 normal size squid
Maldon sea salt
Lime wedges, for squeezing

1 In a mini food-processor or, if you have the energy, a pestle and mortar, bash all the marinade ingredients to a paste. Add a pinch of salt. This is your marinade and it will keep in the fridge as long as it is covered with extra oil to stop the air getting to it.

2 To prepare the squid, start by removing the wings on either side of the body by pulling them away. As you do this, some of the outer membrane should also come off; you need to ensure you remove it all. Then pull down on the tentacles, they should easily come away from the tube-shaped body. When you pull this, all the innards will also come away. You can't eat these, so cut off anything above the tentacles and discard them. Lastly, there is a clear, plastic-looking 'feather' inside the body; this is the backbone and you discard that too.

3 Slice the squid in half, opening it out like a book, and wash thoroughly. Cut down the remaining fold to give you two pieces from each squid. Now score the squid on the inside with a knife, ensuring you don't cut all the way through. Scoring the flesh allows you to tell when the squid is done since it will curl up when cooked to perfection. It also looks really good!

4 Place the prepared squid in the marinade for a minimum of 20 minutes but no longer than 1 hour or the flavour will be too strong. Heat a griddle or a barbecue, and put on the tentacles first. 30 seconds later put on the rest, scored-side down. Cooking will take no more than 2 minutes. Season with Maldon sea salt and a squeeze of lime.

griddled marinated chicken

with a mango, watercress and cashew salad & light thai dipping sauce

SERVES 2

2 chicken breasts, cut into strips
1 garlic clove, crushed
1cm knob of ginger, peeled and crushed
2 teaspoons soy sauce
Zest of 1 lemon
1 teaspoon sugar

FOR THE SALAD
Spring onions, sliced on the angle
1 fresh red chilli, cut into julienne strips
1 large mango, peeled and cut into thin strips but
    not too small
A bunch of fresh coriander, leaves picked
100g cashew nuts, lightly toasted

A bunch of watercress, washed
1 cucumber, cut into julienne strips

FOR THE DIPPING SAUCE
4 tablespoons Thai fish sauce (nam pla)
1 teaspoon dried crushed red chilli
1 garlic clove, finely chopped
1 tablespoon lime juice
1 tablespoon sugar

TO SERVE
Pinch of sugar
Pinch of salt
Lime wedges
Satay sticks, pre-soaked

1 Soak the satay sticks overnight or at least for a few hours to stop them burning on the griddle or barbecue.

2 Put the chicken strips into a bowl with the garlic, ginger, soy sauce, lemon zest and sugar. Leave it to marinate in a cool place for between 20 minutes and 2 hours.

3 Prepare the salad while you preheat a griddle or barbecue by combining all the salad ingredients.

4 Combine all the ingredients for the dipping sauce in a small dish.

5 Thread the chicken onto the pre-soaked satay sticks. Cook the chicken on the griddle or barbecue for 2–3 minutes on each side. Add a pinch of sugar and salt and a squeeze of lime to the salad. Serve the chicken with the salad and dipping sauce.

barbecued leg of lamb

This makes a fab and slightly more sophisticated alternative to boring kebabs and burnt bangers on a lovely, hot summer's day. Leg of lamb is good value when you consider that it will usually feed up to 8 people and is packed full of flavour. You can use any leftovers to make a pickle sandwich for lunch the following day.

Although a lot of supermarkets already sell it this way, you may need to ask your butcher to butterfly the leg of lamb for you. This means removing the bone from the leg and opening out the meat to the same thickness, allowing it to cook evenly. The marinade helps to tenderise the meat as well as adding tasty flavours.

SERVES 6-8

FOR THE MARINADE
Zest and juice of 2 lemons
6 anchovy fillets in oil, drained and finely chopped
1 teaspoon cumin seeds
1 teaspoon fennel seeds

Leaves stripped from 2 sprigs of thyme
1 fresh red chilli, seeds in, chopped
100ml olive oil
2–3 big pinches of salt

1 leg of lamb, weighing about 1.5kg

1 Put all the prepared ingredients for the marinade in a bowl, pour in the oil and add the pinches of salt.

2 Place the butterflied lamb on a baking tray and rub over the marinade. Leave to marinate in the fridge for anything between 20 minutes and 24 hours. The longer you leave it, the deeper the flavours.

3 Heat the barbecue until the coals start to glow white. Lay the lamb straight onto the bars and allow to cook for 12 minutes on each side for medium rare, or for 15–18 minutes on each side for well-done.

Baste the meat with any leftover marinade during the cooking.

4 Remove from the barbecue and allow to rest for 5 minutes so that all the juices relax back into the meat, making it deliciously moist.

5 Carve into thick slices and serve. Perfect with big, barbecued garlic Portobello mushrooms and grilled cherry tomatoes.

 TIP Remove the lamb from the fridge 20 minutes before cooking. This will allow it to come to room temperature, reducing the amount of time necessary for cooking and ensuring the meat cooks more evenly.

char-grilled pomegranate glazed poussin

with carrot and pomegranate salad

This is a lovely recipe to make for a big outside dinner. It's fresh, light and healthy. The colours are beautiful and vibrant, speckled with the little ruby-like pomegranate seeds. Poussin is the French name for baby chicken. Allow one per person or just half each for a light lunch.

SERVES 4 FOR LUNCH

2–4 poussin. Ask your butcher or meat counter to cut it into 4 pieces on the bone

FOR THE MARINADE
50ml orange juice
50ml pomegranate juice
50ml olive oil
1 tablespoon caster sugar
½ teaspoon ground cinnamon
1 teaspoon salt

FOR THE SALAD
3 large carrots, peeled into ribbons using a
    speed peeler
1 medium red chilli, deseeded and sliced

3 spring onions, cut on the angle
1 large pomegranate
½ bunch of flat leaf parsley, leaves only
2 large handfuls of ruby or baby red chard

FOR THE DRESSING
Juice of 1 lime
1 clove garlic, grated
1cm knob of ginger, peeled and grated on a
    microfine grater
1½ teaspoons sugar
1 tablespoon olive oil
Pinch of salt
1 tablespoon pomegranate juice

Handful of toasted peanuts, crushed

1 Prepare the marinade by mixing the ingredients in a large bowl. Massage it into the poussin pieces and leave to marinate for at least 20 minutes, but overnight in the fridge is fine.

2 Make the salad. Put the carrot ribbons, the chilli and the spring onion into a large salad bowl and mix through. Remove the seeds from the pomegranate (I find it easiest to cut it in half and hit it with the back of a spoon). Add to the bowl with the parsley and chard. Give it a good mix around but don't dress the salad until you are ready to serve.

3 Preheat the oven to 180°C/350°F/Gas Mark 4. Heat a griddle pan and lay the poussin on, skin-side down. When griddle lines start to appear, remove from the heat, place on a tray and transfer to the oven for about 12–15 minutes.

4 Make the salad dressing by mixing together all the ingredients and pouring it over the salad. Sprinkle with the toasted peanuts and serve with the chicken.

76

summer one-pot chicken

What's great about this recipe is that it can be adapted so easily depending on what ingredients you like. It's wholesome, healthy and, best of all, it cooks in one big pot. Who has time for washing up? Try to get your hands on corn-fed organic chicken. I know everyone raves about it, but it really is the best. Ask your butchers to cut a whole chicken down for sauté. If they don't know what you mean, find a new butcher. It means to break the chicken down to 8 pieces.

SERVES 4

1 whole medium chicken or 10 thighs
100g seasoned flour
1 tablespoon good-quality olive oil
½ bottle of any dry white wine you have lying about
1 bay leaf
2 sprigs of thyme
Zest of ½ lemon
2 garlic cloves
Salt and freshly ground black pepper

6 baby new potatoes, skin on, halved
4 baby fennel, halved lengthways, or 1 large fennel
   bulb cut into 10 pieces through the root
1 leek, sliced into 1cm rings
1 large white onion, cut into 6, root intact
8 baby carrots, whole
50g peas, fresh or frozen
225g baby spinach, to serve

1 Preheat the oven to 180ºC/350ºF/Gas Mark 4.

2 Lightly dust the chicken pieces or thighs with seasoned flour, thinly coating them. Shake off the surplus.

3 Heat the olive oil in a heavy-based ovenproof pan large enough to fit in the chicken comfortably. Lay the floured chicken pieces in the pan, skin-side down and brown all over. Pour in the wine, add the bay leaf, thyme, lemon zest, garlic, seasoning and enough water to cover the chicken. Bring to the boil. Cover the pan with a lid or tin foil, and put into the preheated oven for 20 minutes.

4 Remove from the oven and add all the root vegetables. Replace the lid and cook for a further 20 minutes. Test with a knife to check that the veg is cooked. Add the peas and cook for a further 5 minutes.

5 To serve, place a handful of the spinach leaves in the bottom of each serving bowl and spoon the casserole over top, allowing the leaves to wilt. Serve with crusty bread to mop up all the delicious juices. Enjoy.

whole seabream

with fennel & lemon

Barbecued whole fish is one of the most wonderful and satisfying things to eat. It's not only really good for you, it's quick, looks great and is quite easy to prepare. I think it's so boring that in the UK in particular a barbie usually consists of only sausages, ribs and burgers. None of these actually cook well on the barbecue and quite often people are still hungry because cremated bangers don't really appeal.

SERVES 4

4 whole seabream, scaled and gutted (ask your fishmonger to do this)
1 lemon, cut into 8 slices
1 bulb of fennel, halved and thinly sliced

4 bay leaves
A bunch of flat leaf parsley
2 tablespoons oil
100ml white wine
Salt and freshly ground black pepper

1 Firstly, ask someone to light the barbecue. (This should never be the chef's job unless of course the person who does it becomes more of a hindrance than a help and it's actually quicker to do it yourself! Or is that just in my house?) It needs to be really hot before you start the cooking.

2 Open the cavity of the fish and rinse under cold running water. Stuff the cavities with equal amounts of lemon and fennel slices, tuck in a bay leaf and a share of the parsley. These flavourings also encourage the fish to steam and remain moist. Season the fish inside and out with salt and pepper.

3 Prepare a double-thick layer of tin foil, big enough to wrap each fish separately. Lay a square of greaseproof paper on top to stop the skin of the fish sticking to the foil.

4 Place the fish in the middle of the greaseproof paper and drizzle with oil. Bring the four corners of foil to the centre to tightly enclose the fish. Leave a small hole, pour in a splash of white wine then close all the gaps. Do the same with the remaining fish.

5 When the barbecue coals are glowing white, place the fishy parcels on the grill. If your barbecue has a lid, put it on now. Turn the parcels after 4–5 minutes, or if they are large fish, give them an extra few minutes. Cook the fish on the second side for 4 minutes then remove from the heat and allow to rest for a few minutes. Serve straight from the foil parcel.

lemon & lime semifreddo

Semifreddo is the best option when it comes to making ice-creamy things at home without the aid of an ice-cream maker. You can put in what you like, but I like to keep it simple. The great thing about this recipe is that it can be jazzed up with a splash of booze if you fancy it. Go easy, however, because if you add too much it will stop the semifreddo setting.

If you want to serve it in slices, you will need a loaf tin or a terrine mould lined with clingfilm. If not, a bowl will be fine and it can be scooped out when set.

SERVES 4–6

Zest of 4 lemons and the juice of 2
Zest and juice of 3 limes
500ml double cream

4 eggs, carefully separated
75g caster sugar
Salt
Gin or vodka (optional), no more than 50ml
Fresh berry fruit, to serve

1 Zest and juice your lemons and limes and set aside. Lightly whip the double cream until soft peaks form. Whisk the egg yolks and sugar until pale and fold in the cream.

2 In another clean bowl (I rub mine with a lemon to remove any trace of grease), whisk the egg whites with a tiny pinch of salt until they form a meringue. Using a metal spoon, gently fold the egg whites quarter by quarter into the cream. When everything is combined, add in the zest and juice.

3 For a kick, add a splash of gin or vodka. Pour into your mould and leave to set in the freezer for about 2 hours. Serve as slices or scoops with fresh berries.

'pick me up' tiramisu

Tiramisu is a very grown-up dessert; I'm yet to find a child who will eat the whole thing and not just the top bit. Remember, as it's very rich, you don't need much, so serve in small glasses.

MAKES 6–8 GLASSES

10 amaretti biscuits, crushed
100ml Marsala
2 double espressos or very strong coffee

3 egg yolks
100g icing sugar
250g mascarpone
Cocoa powder, for dusting

1 Place the amaretti biscuits in the bottom of your serving glasses. Using only half of it, spoon over equal amounts of Marsala and coffee. It should taste boozy and strong.

2 Cream together the egg yolks and icing sugar. Beat the mascarpone with the remaining Marsala and coffee and fold into the egg and sugar mix.

3 Fill up the glasses and smooth the tops of the glasses. Chill for a few hours before you serve, dust with the cocoa powder at the last minute.

itsy bitsy teeny weeny trifles

Slightly old-fashioned and yes, I admit, slightly tacky BUT everyone loves trifle and no one will be able refuse these individual servings. If you've already made a trifle you'll know that it always looks irresistible in its lovely layers, but then becomes disastrous when served. So here I've made individual ones. Don't be afraid to be inventive with your serving glasses. Visit a party shop and buy different plastic glasses, beakers or containers, or look in your glasses cupboard: cocktail or shot glasses are great.

MAKES 5–6 SHOT GLASSES

100ml fresh whipping cream
50g sugar
Seeds scraped from 1 vanilla pod
¼ Madeira cake, chopped and crumbled

50ml Madeira or sweet sherry, plus extra for sprinkling
Strawberry jam, either homemade (see page 57)
   or shop-bought
100ml custard, either homemade (see page 156)
   or shop-bought
125g raspberries or any fresh berries you fancy

1 Whip the cream with the sugar and the vanilla seeds. If you intend to make your own custard, reserve the pod to flavour the milk. If not, drop it into a jar of sugar to flavour.

2 Crumble the Madeira cake into the bottom of the glasses. Douse the cake with a little Madeira or sherry, about a tablespoon in each glass. Top with a teaspoon of strawberry jam then spoon on the

thick custard. Add a few berries and sprinkle over a little more Madeira. Finish with a layer of sweetened cream.

3 Smooth over the top of the glass and decorate with whatever you fancy, maybe a few berries and some mint.

sozzled berry jelly

If you happen to have guests who prefer boozy fruits to luscious cream, then this is the dessert for them.

MAKES 6–8 SHOT GLASSES

2 gelatine leaves
50ml crème de cassis or any berry liqueur that
 happens to be lurking in your cupboard
50ml vodka

200ml apple juice
200g caster sugar
6 strawberries
10 raspberries
10 blueberries

1 Soften the gelatine in a little cold water for 20 minutes.

2 Gently heat the crème de cassis and vodka with the apple juice and sugar just long enough to dissolve the sugar. Add the gelatine and allow to melt. Pass the mixture through a sieve to catch any bits that don't completely melt.

3 Put the fruit in your chosen glasses and pour over the warm unset liquid. Carefully place in the fridge and leave to set for 3–4 hours. They'll keep for up to 4 days.

peach & basil granita

This is a great summertime option for a quick palate-cleanser or a refreshing alternative to sorbet if you don't have an ice-cream churner. Tinned peaches, preferably in juice not syrup, are best to use for this recipe.

SERVES 4

500ml peach purée made from tinned,
   drained peaches
160g caster sugar

50ml water
Juice of 1 lemon
1 packet basil, a few leaves reserved for decoration

1 To make the purée, simply whizz the peaches in a food-processor.

2 Bring the sugar, water, lemon juice and basil slowly to the boil to dissolve the sugar but do not allow it to colour. Leave to cool. The basil will infuse into the syrup.

3 Add the cooled syrup to the purée and mix thoroughly. Pour into a plastic tub or container and place in the freezer. Every half hour or so, fork through to break up the ice crystals as they form.

4 After 2–3 hours, when all is set and the particles are separate, get serving! Decorate with the reserved basil.

winter warmers

These are my favourite comfort foods – warming, hearty and utterly wonderful at keeping the cold weather at bay. Use your favourite childhood recipes as inspiration. These are the types of recipes that fill the house with delicious smells and get everyone's bellies rumbling, so get ready to dish out some big portions.

winter veg

Doing something even slightly different with your traditional winter veggies can always be a bit of a risk. We all know it's easy just to roast your spuds and boil your cabbage, but why not try doing something a little unusual, possibly more adventurous and definitely more tasty?

roasted parsnips

These are quicker to prepare – not to mention healthier – than traditional roast potatoes.

SERVES 6

6–8 parsnips
2 tablespoons olive oil

Salt and freshly ground black pepper
2 tablespoons honey

1 Preheat the oven to 190°C/375°F/Gas Mark 5.

2 Peel the parsnips and cut each one in half, then into quarters, then in half again. Remove and discard the woody core from each piece.

3 Place the parsnips on a baking tray and pour over the oil, salt, pepper and honey. Stir to ensure all the pieces are well coated. Transfer the tray to the oven for 15–20 minutes until the parsnips are golden brown and crispy.

TIP Select smaller parsnips because these will be sweeter than the big ones and less woody in the middle, meaning less wastage.

cauliflower fritters

Everyone agrees that cauliflower cheese is delicious, but this recipe gives you a lovely variation. Enjoy alongside a roast dinner or as a great veggie starter.

MAKES ABOUT 16 FRITTERS

½ large cauliflower, cut into florets
60g plain flour
1 teaspoon baking powder
60g Cheddar or gruyère cheese

½ teaspoon grated nutmeg
½ teaspoon dried red chilli
Salt and freshly ground black pepper
2 whole eggs
500ml vegetable oil for deep-frying

1 Drop the cauliflower into boiling water and cook until just tender. Don't let it go soggy, slightly under-cooked is great because you want the fritters to have a bit of texture.

2 Drain and rinse the florets under cold water to stop the cooking process. Chop them into smallish chunks and place in a bowl.

3 Sift the flour and the baking powder into a mixing bowl and add the cheese, nutmeg and chilli. Season. Make a well in the centre and drop in the eggs. Slowly mix with a wooden spoon until it is all incorporated and most of the lumps have gone. Fold in the cauliflower florets and coat thoroughly in the batter.

4 Heat the oil, preferably in a deep-fat fryer, to 170ºC. If you don't have one, heat the oil in a deep-sided pan. It will be at the correct temperature if you drop in a piece of bread and it bubbles instantly.

5 Take a tablespoonful of the mix and slide it into the fryer, using another spoon to push the mix off if it helps. Always work away from you when deep-frying. Fry the fritters until golden brown and remove from the oil. Place on absorbent paper, sprinkle with salt and serve.

 TIP Only fill the pan slightly less than halfway with oil and never try to cook too much in the pan; always deep-fry in batches.

celeriac dauphinoise

SERVES 4–5

Butter, for greasing
2 celeriac roots, peeled
300ml double cream

50g butter, plus extra for greasing
2 garlic cloves, thinly sliced
Leaves stripped from 2 sprigs of fresh thyme
Salt and freshly ground black pepper

1 Preheat oven to 180°C/350°F/Gas Mark 4. Grease a baking dish with sides 5cm deep with butter.

2 Slice the celeriac as thinly as possible. Take your time doing this. If you have a mandoline, this is perfect for the job but it's not essential.

3 Place the cream and the butter in a pan, heat to simmering point then remove from the hob.

4 Now spoon a layer of cream into the bottom of the baking dish, followed by a layer of celeriac slices, a little of the garlic and a few thyme leaves.

Spoon on some more cream, season well with salt and pepper and repeat the process again. You should manage about 4–5 layers. Each time you form a new layer, ensure it is well pressed down.

5 When you have used all the celeriac, pour over the remaining cream and season again. Sprinkle over a few thyme leaves.

6 Put the baking dish in the oven for 1–1½ hours. If the top starts to look too coloured, simply cover the dish with foil or baking parchment. Pierce with a knife to check the celeriac is cooked in the middle. Serve piping hot.

balsamic roasted beetroot

Beetroot, believe it or not, isn't just something you buy pickled, peeled and vac-packed from the supermarket. If you buy it raw, there are lots of different ways of preparing it. Its very subtle, earthy flavour goes fantastically with strong, hearty meats.

SERVES 6

6 large uncooked beetroot, leaves trimmed but allow
   a tuft of stalk to remain
100ml balsamic vinegar
100ml olive oil, plus extra for drizzling
6 sprigs of thyme
Maldon sea salt and freshly ground black pepper

1 Preheat the oven to 160°C/325°F/Gas Mark 3.

2 Cut out six 20cm squares of tin foil. Place one beetroot in the centre of each square and pour over 1 tablespoon of the balsamic and 1 tablespoon of the olive oil. Add a sprig of thyme. Season with plenty of salt and lots of black pepper.

3 Wrap them up tightly in the foil making a closed parcel and place on a baking tray. Transfer to the oven and cook for about 1½ hours. Insert a sharp knife into a beetroot to see whether it is cooked. It won't be as tender as a potato would be, but not far off.

4 To serve, open up the foil, slit the top of the beetroot and drizzle with extra olive oil.

creamy savoy cabbage & smoked bacon

The perfect combo.

SERVES 6

1 whole Savoy cabbage
50g unsalted butter
100g smoked pancetta lardons or smoked streaky
   bacon, diced
75ml double cream
Salt and freshly ground black pepper
50g cooked chestnuts (sold vacuum-packed),
   roughly chopped

1 Only remove the tough outer leaves of the cabbage if they look beaten up. If not, you can cook them too. Finely slice the cabbage by first cutting it in half, then into quarters and slicing them to the root.

2 Heat the butter in a large frying pan and fry off the bacon or pancetta, until it starts to turn golden brown. Add in the cabbage with a splash of water and allow to steam and wilt for a few minutes. Don't cover the pan or your cabbage will go brown.

3 When the cabbage has started to cook down, add the cream and plenty of seasoning.

4 Reduce the cream for a further few minutes until no liquid remains and finally add the chestnuts.

duck & plum autumn salad

For me, this salad represents autumn. It couldn't be easier and the beauty is that you can use leftover roast duck or just roast a couple of legs which have such a fantastic rich flavour and are completely underused. The plums in the salad complement the rich duck and bring a warm component to the dish.

SERVES 4

FOR THE MARINADE
4 cloves
1 cinnamon stick
2 star anise
6 peppercorns
4 juniper berries
1 teaspoon salt

4 duck legs, skin on

2 tablespoons honey
2 tablespoons olive oil
300ml red wine
100g sugar
6 plums, not too ripe, halved and stoned
2 tablespoons balsamic vinegar
Mixture of autumn salad leaves such as radicchio, mizuna, oak leaf, purple basil, red or ruby chard, chervil, rocket
Salt and freshly ground black pepper
75g walnut halves

1 Preheat the oven to 160°C/325°F/Gas Mark 3.

2 Make a dry marinade by crushing half the quantity of each of the spices (the rest go into the poaching broth) with 1 teaspoon of salt in a pestle and mortar. Place the duck legs in a roasting tin and rub with 1 tablespoon of the honey and all the oil then sprinkle on the fragrant dry marinade.

3 Transfer to the oven for about 2 hours until tender. If the duck starts to look a little dry, add a splash of red wine to create some steam.

4 To make the poaching liquor, pour the wine into a saucepan and add the remaining half of the spices and the sugar. Put the plums into the pan and poach slowly for about 20 minutes. They should still be quite firm but will have taken on the colour and flavour of the liquor. Remove the pan from the heat

but leave the plums to cool in the liquor until the duck is ready.

5 When the duck is cooked, remove from the tray and allow to cool a little.

6 Put the roasting tray on the hob and deglaze with a little of the poaching liquor, scraping up all the bits from the base of the pan. Add the remaining tablespoon of honey and the balsamic vinegar.

7 Allow to cool a little while you shred the duckmeat off the bone. Include the crispy skin in the salad.

8 Mix the duck through gently with your leaves, dress with the warm dressing and season. Pile on the plates, sprinkle with the walnut halves and arrange the plums around the edge.

braised beef chuck

This stew really is the ideal winter warmer and makes a great family dinner; there is really no point in making this dish for just two people. You're going to need a big casserole dish – one that you can use on the hob and put into the oven is ideal – and you want to cook it as slowly as possible for maximum flavour and tenderness. If you prepare it during the day, all you have to do is throw it in the oven and lay the table ready for a delicious evening meal.

SERVES 6–8

100g seasoned flour
1.5kg beef chuck, cut into 200–225g portions
50ml vegetable oil, for frying in batches
½ bottle of red wine, goodish quality (if you won't drink it, don't cook with it!)
4 sprigs of thyme
4 bay leaves
5 juniper berries

1 whole bulb of garlic, cut in half horizontally
1 litre brown stock, made from a cube is fine
2 tablespoons Worcestershire sauce
6 shallots, peeled and halved
2 carrots, peeled and cut into 3 or 4 depending on size
1 leek, cut to the same size as your carrots
2 celery sticks, cut to the same size as your carrots
Salt and freshly ground black pepper

1 Put the seasoned flour on a plate and use it to lightly coat the meat pieces on all sides, shaking off the excess. Heat your pan with the oil and put the meat into the hot oil to seal. If the pieces don't all fit in the base of the pan, work in batches because you're aiming to get a good amount of colour over all the meat.

2 When all the meat is sealed, remove it from the pan. Pour in the red wine to deglaze the pan and scrape off all the bits from the base of the pan – these are great for flavour.

3 Return the meat to the pan, together with the thyme, bay leaves, juniper berries, garlic, stock and the Worcestershire sauce. Bring to the boil and place a lid on.

4 You can cook this on a very low heat either on the hob or in the oven at 160ºC/325ºF/Gas Mark 3.

5 After 2½–3 hours, add in the prepared vegetables and cook for a further 1–1½ hours. Check periodically and if the stock is looking a bit low and no longer covering the meat and veg, add a touch more.

6 At the end of cooking, check the seasoning. This is best served with a creamy mash and Roasted Parsnips (see page 88).

TIP As with all stews and casseroles, this gets better with age as the flavours start to intensify. It's perfectly fine to cook this dish 2 or 3 days in advance provided you store it correctly (in the fridge, clingwrapped).

maple-glazed ham hock

Ham hocks are cheap as chips, really tender and totally addictive and yet they are an extremely under-used and neglected cut of scrumptious meat. (In case you didn't know, ham hock comes from the ankle of the pig.) I find it frustrating that most supermarkets don't stock produce like this; you will have to go to a good butcher.

**SERVES 3–4
(WITH SOME LEFT OVER FOR THE
PICCALILLI SANDWICHES – PAGE 42)**

2 ham hocks
2 carrots
1 celery stick
1 onion

4 cloves
2 bay leaves
4 peppercorns

FOR THE STICKY GLAZE
1 tablespoon Dijon mustard
125ml maple syrup
1 teaspoon ground cinnamon
1 teaspoon ground cloves

1 Cover the ham hocks in cold water and leave to soak for at least an hour (overnight is better), changing the water at least once if you can.

2 Cut the vegetables (unpeeled) into 5cm pieces. Put the soaked ham hocks into a big saucepan, add the vegetables, the spices and herbs. Cover with water and place on the hob. Gently bring to the boil, removing any scum that collects with a slotted spoon. Cook the hocks for 3 hours or until the meat is falling off the bone.

3 Preheat the oven to 200°C/400°F/Gas Mark 6.

4 Remove the hocks carefully from the water and lay on a baking tray to cool slightly. Remove the thick layer of fat if you can and lightly brush the outside of the meat with the Dijon mustard. Pour over the maple syrup and sprinkle with the ground cinnamon and cloves.

5 Transfer to the oven and bake for about 15 minutes or until the maple has caramelised. Remove from the oven and allow to cool slightly before pulling the meat from the bone.

6 This is perfect served with Cinnamon Roasted Quince (see page 105) and some crispy, fresh peppery salad leaves such as mizuna.

slow-cooked shoulder of lamb

with flageolet beans

This is so easy to prepare, in fact, there's not really anything to prepare at all! I love this because it makes a change to the usual Sunday lunch. It really couldn't be easier. A one-pot wonder.

Shoulder of lamb, even when it's of really good quality, isn't expensive and goes a long way if you're feeding a big family. It should be cooked long and slow, as should most good winter warmers.

SERVES 6–8

2 tablespoons olive oil

1 whole shoulder of lamb, bone in (that's where all the flavour is)

2 white onions, cut into eighths through the root

1 bulb of garlic, cut in half horizontally

½ bottle white wine

1 litre chicken, lamb or vegetable stock

2 bay leaves

Zest of 2 lemons, grated on a microfine grater

4 peppercorns

3 sprigs of rosemary

800g tinned flageolet beans

400g tinned cannellini beans

Salt and freshly ground black pepper

1 Preheat the oven to 160°C/325°F/Gas Mark 3.

2 Heat the olive oil in a large ovenproof casserole. Season the lamb all over and seal in the pan until golden brown on all sides. Remove the meat and likewise seal the onions and the garlic.

3 Deglaze the pan with the white wine then add the meat back into the pan. Bring to the boil and add the stock. Return to the boil and remove any scum that may come to the surface with a slotted spoon.

4 Now add the bay leaves, lemon zest, peppercorns and rosemary. Cover the casserole with its lid or with tin foil and place in the oven for 2½–3 hours. Check periodically to ensure the meat is covered; if not, just add a little more wine or stock, or baste well.

5 Remove the casserole from the oven and stir in the beans. Cook for a further 30 minutes with the lid off.

6 Discard the garlic. Serve with bright green vegetables.

suet pastry game pudding

SERVES 6

Butter, for greasing
400g lean game meat (venison, pheasant, partridge),
    boned weight
2 skinned and boned chicken thighs
Salt and freshly ground black pepper
2 tablespoons plain flour
1 white onion, sliced
1 garlic clove, crushed
4 juniper berries, crushed
1 tablespoon chopped parsley

1 small bay leaf
1 tablespoon Worcestershire sauce
½ small glass of red wine
200ml beef stock, cooled

FOR THE SUET PASTRY
Butter, for greasing
175g suet
1 teaspoon turmeric
350g self-raising flour
Salt and freshly ground black pepper
A few drops of cold water

1 Butter a 1 litre pudding basin well, and line the base with a disc of baking parchment.

2 Put the suet into a mixing bowl, sift over the turmeric and flour. Season with a little salt and pepper. Add a few drops of cold water and mix in with your hands. Continue adding a few drops until there is just enough to combine the mixture to form a dough. Turn out and knead the dough until smooth and elastic. This should take a few minutes.

3 Cut out a quarter of the pastry and roll the rest to 0.5cm thick. Use this to line the greased pudding basin, allowing some to overhang the edges. Roll out the remaining quarter into a disc the size of the top of the pudding basin and reserve.

4 Put the meats in a mixing bowl, season with salt and pepper and coat in the flour. Mix in the onion, garlic, juniper berries, parsley, bay leaf and Worcestershire sauce. Spoon this mixture into the lined basin, pour over the wine and cover with the cold stock. The filling will look thin and strange at this point, but don't worry.

5 Wet the pastry that forms the rim of the pudding and place the pastry lid on top. Press down all the way around to ensure it is well sealed and trim off the excess. Cover the pudding with a disc of baking parchment and a double layer of pleated foil. Secure tightly under the rim of the basin with string.

6 Make a steamer by placing an upturned ceramic saucer in a large saucepan. Pour enough boiling water into the pan to come halfway up the sides and lower the pudding onto the saucer. Cover with a tight-fitting lid. Steam for 3 hours over a low heat, topping up the pan with hot water so it doesn't boil dry. Don't let the water boil rapidly.

7 Lift the pudding out of the steamer and let it stand for 10 minutes. Remove the foil and paper, cover the base with a plate and invert the pudding. Gently remove the basin to reveal your beautifully moist pudding! Cut into portions and serve.

spiced butter biscuits, roasted figs & cinnamon ice cream

There are three separate steps to this recipe but two of them can be done up to a week in advance, just leaving the figs to be prepared last minute.

spiced butter biscuits

MAKES 10–12 BISCUITS

125g butter, softened
60g caster sugar, plus extra for dusting
180g plain flour, plus extra for rolling
½ teaspoon ground cinnamon
½ teaspoon ground ginger
½ teaspoon ground allspice

1 Preheat the oven to 180°C/350°F/Gas Mark 4. Line a baking tray with baking parchment, unless you have a non-stick one.

2 Cream together the butter and sugar until light and fluffy.

3 Sift together all the dry ingredients and beat them into the creamed mixture. Lightly flour the work surface, turn out the mixture and bring it together in a ball. Leave to harden slightly in the fridge for 20 minutes.

4 Flour your rolling pin and roll out the dough to a thickness of about 1cm.

5 Cut into fingers or into rounds with pastry cutters and lay on a baking sheet. Dust with caster sugar and leave to rest in the fridge for 10 minutes.

6 Bake for 15–20 minutes or until golden. Remove and allow to cool completely. These biscuits will keep for a week in an airtight container.

cinnamon ice cream

MAKES 10–12 SERVINGS

290ml double cream
1 cinnamon stick
1 bay leaf
½ teaspoon ground cinnamon
4 egg yolks
115g caster sugar

1 Place the double cream, cinnamon stick, bay leaf and ground cinnamon in a saucepan. Gently bring to a simmer but don't allow to boil.

2 Meanwhile, whisk together the egg yolks and the sugar. Just before the cream boils, gently pour it over the egg mix, stirring continuously so that you don't end up with scrambled eggs.

3 Return the mixture to the pan and cook, stirring, on a low heat for a few minutes until it thickens. It's best to use a rubber spatula. Don't forget to stir right into the edges.

4 Once thickened, strain the mixture through a sieve and leave to cool slightly.

5 This custard is now ready to go into an ice-cream machine if you have one. If you don't, pour it into a bowl or plastic container and transfer to the freezer. Stir the custard every 20–30 minutes until it has set. Once set, cover the bowl with clingfilm. If you ensure the clingfilm touches the surface of the ice cream, ice crystals won't form on top.

roasted figs

SERVES 5

10 ripe fresh figs
10 teaspoons honey
Zest and juice of 1 orange

1 Preheat the oven to 180°C/350°F/Gas Mark 4.

2 Cut the figs open by cutting a cross in the top of the fig and squeezing from the bottom of the fig to open it up like a flower. Place them in a small baking dish.

3 Spoon a teaspoon of honey into each fruit, along with a pinch of orange zest. Squeeze the orange juice into the baking dish and transfer to the oven. Cook for 10–12 minutes, basting the figs halfway through cooking to keep them moist and juicy.

4 To serve, place a hot fig on each plate with a couple of scoops of ice cream and biscuits on the side.

real lemon meringue pie

This is a dessert that I remember my Mum making on a Sunday when my Nana used to come for lunch. She really loved it, so I would like to dedicate this one to her.

MAKES A 22–25CM PIE

1 x Shortcrust Pastry recipe (see p 156)
Butter, for greasing
Flour, for rolling

FOR THE FILLING
2½ tablespoons cornflour
260ml water

50g caster sugar
Zest and juice of 3 lemons
3 egg yolks (reserve the whites for the meringue)
50g butter

FOR THE MERINGUE
3 egg whites
180g caster sugar

1 Preheat the oven to 190°C/375°F/Gas Mark 5. Grease the pie dish with butter.

2 Remove the pastry from the fridge and roll out on a lightly floured surface until it forms a round slightly bigger than your dish. Roll the rolled pastry over your rolling pin and lay into the pie dish. Carefully push in around the edges ensuring there is no air trapped between the dish and the pastry.

3 Trim up the edges, prick the base with a fork and allow to rest in the fridge for a further 20 minutes. Line the pastry with baking parchment and baking beans. Bake in the oven for 12 minutes or until lightly golden brown. Remove the parchment and baking beans and cook for a further 5 minutes.

4 Meanwhile, make the filling. Mix the cornflour and a little of the water to make a smooth paste. Put the sugar, the remaining water and lemon zest in a small pan. Bring to the boil. Slowly pour in the

cornflour mix, return to the heat and keep stirring until it starts to thicken. Remove from the heat once it is the consistency of double cream.

5 Whisk together the egg yolks, lemon juice and butter. Slowly pour the hot mix over the eggs, whisking constantly. Pour into the pastry case.

6 To make the meringue, take a clean bowl and ensure it is grease-free by rubbing the bowl with a cut lemon. Whisk the egg whites to soft peaks then slowly add the sugar and continue to whisk until a meringue forms.

7 Pile the meringue on top of the lemon curd and smooth the edges with a pallet knife. Make little peaks in the meringue with a fork and bake for 45 minutes until it is lightly golden and crisp.

8 Leave to cool before serving.

bread pudding

Although it sounds similar, this is not bread and butter pudding. It's fruity, spicy, gooey and sweet all at once – possibly the most moist and delectable pudding I've ever tasted.

SERVES 6 GENEROUSLY

Butter, for greasing
150g plump sultanas
50ml brandy
1 slice of brown bread, crusts removed
   (stale bread is fine)
275ml milk
50g candied orange peel
25g candied lemon peel

50g melted butter
80g dark soft brown sugar (muscovado is perfect)
1 egg
Zest of 1 lemon
Zest of 1 orange
50g demerara sugar
1 teaspoon ground cinnamon
1 teaspoon ground cloves
1 teaspoon mixed spice
1 teaspoon ground ginger

1 Preheat the oven to 180°C/350°F/Gas Mark 4. Grease a baking dish measuring about 15 x 20cm and 5cm deep.

2 First soak the sultanas in the brandy. Roughly tear the bread into 1–2cm pieces and pour over the milk. Leave until the bread has soaked up all the milk.

3 Combine all the remaining ingredients in a large mixing bowl, including the soaked raisins and brandy. Once combined, mix in the soaked bread.

4 Pour into the greased baking dish and cook for about 1–1½ hours. Serve out of the dish while still hot. It has to be served with piping hot custard (see page 156).

cinnamon-roasted quince

SERVES 3–4

2 quinces
75g butter
100ml white wine

2 tablespoons maple syrup
1 teaspoon ground cinnamon
4 cloves
Zest of 1 orange

1 Preheat the oven to 180°C/350°F/Gas Mark 4.

2 Peel the quinces. Halve and remove the core using a melon baller or a teaspoon.

3 Place the quinces on a baking tray with a knob of butter in the centre of each one. Add the white wine

to the bottom of the tray. Drizzle maple syrup over the quince, put a pinch of cinnamon on each one, stud each with a clove and add the orange zest.

4 Cover the tray with foil and place in the oven for 12–15 minutes or until the quince are soft when tested with the point of a sharp knife.

fast feasts

Whatever your relationship with cooking, sometimes we simply need it fast and easy. This chapter will hopefully suit everyone's needs, whether you live alone or have a large hungry family to feed. These recipes are simple and will take minimal time and effort. The ingredients are straightforward and won't have you running all over town. In fact it's always wise to get your ingredients before the day of cooking; there's nothing like a trip to the supermarket after a long day at work to turn anyone towards the ready-meal aisle.

paella

Paella looks and tastes fantastic – especially if you've got a huge flat paella pan to act as both cooking and serving dish. If you haven't, then use the widest-based pan you have to ensure the rice has the chance to cook evenly. The only slightly difficult part of paella is planning the ingredients but once you've got that list written, it's plain sailing! Remember, with paella you can choose what you like and leave out what you don't.

SERVES 4

1 tablespoon vegetable oil
4 boneless chicken thighs, seasoned
2 shallots, finely chopped
1 red pepper, deseeded and chopped
3 garlic cloves, peeled and finely chopped
1 medium red chilli, deseeded (if you prefer) and
  finely chopped
200g chorizo sausage, diced
1 teaspoon paprika
Pinch of saffron strands

1 tablespoon tomato purée
300g paella rice (or you can use risotto rice)
200ml white wine
1 fish stock cube dissolved in 1 litre hot water
Salt and freshly ground black pepper
100g clams, unshelled
2–3 tubes squid, cleaned and sliced into rings
8 large prawns, shells on
100g mussels, unshelled, cleaned, beards removed
  and any with broken or open shells discarded
50g frozen peas
Squeeze of lemon juice

1 Ensure all your vegetables and the chorizo are prepared before you start.

2 Heat your widest pan with the oil. Place the seasoned chicken thighs skin-side down and leave on the heat until they take on a golden-brown colour. When they're cooked halfway through, remove from the pan and set aside.

3 Add the shallot, pepper, garlic, chilli and chorizo to the pan. Cook for a couple of minutes until the shallots have become translucent. Add the paprika, saffron and tomato purée. Mix well together then add the rice. Stir the rice so that every grain is coated in tomato then add the white wine. When most of the wine has evaporated, return the chicken to the pan and add enough stock to just cover the rice.

Season well and give a little stir to lift some of the rice off the bottom of the pan. Your heat should be quite low now.

4 Cook for 10–12 minutes or until most of the stock has been absorbed then add the seafood. Scatter it over the paella and place the peas on top.

5 Pour over the remaining stock then cover the pan with a lid if you have one, or tightly cover with foil to help the mussels and clams steam open (this takes about 4–6 minutes). If the rice is not quite cooked but the liquid has evaporated, add an extra dash of wine and a squeeze of lemon at this stage and cook a little longer.

6 When the seafood shells are open and the prawns are pink, it's ready to serve.

Try to include saffron if you can. Turmeric will give the dish the right colour but not the same flavour.

109

seared venison loin

with oriental salad

Many people wouldn't think of venison as an everyday meat. It used to have a reputation for being very heavy but farmed venison has developed a very subtle yet rich flavour that works well with salads. The meat is very lean with hardly any cholesterol or fat content so it's healthy and therefore well worth trying.

SERVES 2

1 tablespoon oil
Salt and freshly ground black pepper
300g venison loin (in one piece)

FOR THE SALAD
1 carrot, cut into julienne strips
½ cucumber, cut into julienne strips
¼ mooli (Japanese radish), cut into julienne strips
4 spring onions, cut into julienne strips

A large handful of sprouting mung beans or
    bean sprouts
100ml soy sauce
50ml mirin (Japanese cooking wine)
1 tablespoon sugar
3cm knob of ginger, peeled and finely chopped
1 red chilli, deseeded, finely chopped
Squeeze of lime juice
Coriander leaves

Pumpkin seeds, to garnish

1 Preheat the oven to 180ºC/350ºF/Gas Mark 4. Heat the oil in a frying pan. Season the venison loin with salt and pepper. Sear the meat on all sides, put it on a baking tray and transfer to the oven. Cook for 6–8 minutes – it should be very rare – then leave to rest for 5 minutes.

2 Mix together the carrot, cucumber, mooli, spring onions and mung beans in a large salad bowl. In a small saucepan, gently warm the soy sauce, mirin, sugar, ginger and chilli over a low heat. Add a squeeze of lime, strain and pour over the salad.

3 At the last minute, mix some coriander leaves through the salad. Slice the venison and place on top of the salad. Garnish with pumpkin seeds seasoned with plenty of salt and serve.

TIP Mooli is also known as white radish or daikon. Both mooli and sprouting mung beans are available in Oriental supermarkets.

111

sausages with lentils

This dish is a really quick and flavoursome supper. It's very important to have good-quality sausages for this, especially since they're the main ingredient. Lentils are not used enough at dinner time. I think people are a bit scared of them and unsure how to cook them. The truth is, they're really versatile as well as delicious and will cook in no time at all.

SERVES 4

1 tablespoon vegetable oil
8 sausages
100g smoked lardons or streaky bacon, cut into
    small pieces
1 red onion, thinly sliced
3 garlic cloves, thinly sliced

350g lentils, washed in cold water
1 bay leaf
Sprig of thyme
100ml red wine
500ml vegetable or chicken stock
Salt and freshly ground black pepper

1 Preheat the oven to 180°C/350°F/Gas Mark 4.

2 Heat a cast-iron casserole on the hob and add the oil. When hot, add the sausages and colour on all sides. At this stage you are not cooking them, as they will be popped into the oven later. Remove from the pan and set aside.

3 Add the lardons to the same pan and the onion and garlic. Gently fry. Add the washed lentils to the mix and stir around to coat in the juices. Add the bay leaf, the thyme and a couple of twists of pepper

but no salt at this stage because it makes the lentils toughen up and go hard. Pour in a splash of red wine, allow to bubble until reduced to about half the amount, then add enough stock to cover the lentils.

4 Place the sausages on top of the lentils, cover the pan with a lid or with foil and cook in the oven for 20 minutes. Check after 10 minutes and if the stock is being absorbed too quickly, add another splash.

5 When cooked, season with salt and extra pepper. Serve with broccoli on the side.

my thai green curry

You can make the paste in large batches and as long as you keep it in an airtight container, covered with a layer of oil, it will keep for a good two weeks in the fridge. You can even freeze it in batches, then it will keep for up to three months. This paste is enough for one curry. If you want a big batch, just double or triple it.

SERVES 4 WELL

FOR THE PASTE
1 stick of lemongrass
3 large green chillies, seeds in
5–7cm knob of ginger, peeled
4 garlic cloves
Zest of 1 lime, removed using a speed peeler
Stalks and roots of 1 large bunch of coriander, leaves chopped and reserved for garnishing
1 tablespoon coriander seeds, toasted
1 kaffir lime leaf

FOR THE CURRY
2 tablespoons groundnut oil
6–8 boneless chicken thighs, cubed, or 30 king prawns, shell off
4 spring onions
8 baby corn
1 green pepper
A handful of mangetout
400ml tin of coconut milk
1 teaspoon fish sauce (nam pla)
1 teaspoon soy sauce
Pinch of sugar
Salt

1 To make the paste, roughly chop all the ingredients and place in a food-processor. Pulse to a fine paste. If you're feeling energetic, you can grind it all in a pestle and mortar but that's far too much like hard work for me. If you're having a little trouble getting the paste fine, add a little groundnut oil to the food-processor to loosen it up a bit.

2 Heat a wok or heavy-based pan, add the groundnut oil and fry off the curry paste. When the paste starts to smell really aromatic, add the chicken (if using) and the vegetables (if using prawns, see step 3). Coat everything in the paste by turning for 3–4 minutes. Then add the coconut milk, fish sauce, soy sauce and the sugar. Bring to the boil and cook for 5–6 minutes.

3 If you are using prawns instead of chicken, add them at this stage. At the last minute, stir in the reserved coriander leaves. Serve with boiled Thai jasmine rice.

 TIP The trick to making a stir-fry or curry simple is to have everything ready before you start cooking. Have them laid out in the order you use them too.

113

noodly oriental broth

Oriental-style food tends to not only be really quick to cook, but also full of flavour and quite healthy.

SERVES 2 FOR DINNER OR 3 FOR LUNCH

1.5 litres chicken stock, made from a cube is fine
2.5cm knob of ginger, peeled and finely sliced into strips
1 garlic clove, sliced
1 medium red chilli, finely sliced
2.5cm piece of lemongrass, smashed with the back of your knife
1 tablespoon soy sauce

1 teaspoon fish sauce (nam pla)

2 boneless, skinless chicken breasts
200g soba, buckwheat or glass noodles
1 head of pak choy, cut in half through the root
4 shiitake or chestnut mushrooms
1 handful of beansprouts
Sprigs of coriander, to garnish

1 Start by making a fragrant poaching stock. Place the stock in a pan and bring to the boil. Add the ginger, garlic, half the chilli, lemongrass, soy sauce and fish sauce. Allow to infuse for a couple of minutes.

2 Add the chicken breasts and slowly poach to keep them moist inside. They should take 8–10 minutes, depending on size. Halfway through cooking, add the noodles.

3 Now add the pak choy, and cook for 1 minute, followed by the mushrooms and the beansprouts. Don't over-cook the mushrooms or they will go slimy and spongy.

4 To serve, remove the chicken from the stock and cut into slices to make it easier to eat. Place in big bowls, pour the broth on top, and sprinkle with the reserved chilli. Garnish each bowl with a sprig of coriander.

TIP This dish is also great with crabmeat, prawns and most seafood. It's fab with just vegetables too.

roast chicken

with peas and lettuce

SERVES 4–5

75g butter, softened
½ bunch of fresh chervil, roughly chopped
½ bunch of fresh tarragon, roughly chopped
Zest of 1 lemon
1 free-range chicken, preferably organic
Salt and freshly ground black pepper
½ glass white wine

FOR THE PEAS

150g smoked lardons or bacon rashers, cut into
    small pieces
1 garlic clove
500g frozen petit pois
500ml chicken stock
2 heads of baby gem lettuce, finely shredded
Pinch of sugar
A squeeze of fresh lemon juice
½ bunch of fresh mint, shredded
25g butter and 25g flour, mixed together to make
    a beurre manié

1 Preheat the oven to 180°C/350°F/Gas Mark 4.

2 Take the softened butter and combine it with the chopped herbs and lemon zest. Remove any trussing string from the chicken as this slows down the cooking time and stops the bird cooking as evenly.

3 Releasing the skin on the chicken around the breast with your fingers, push the herb and butter mix under the skin, pushing it as far down the breast as you can.

4 Season the skin with salt and pepper. Be generous, 30 per cent will be lost while cooking. Lay the chicken on its side on a baking tray and place in the oven.

5 After 30 minutes, baste the chicken well, turn it onto the other side to allow even cooking and add a splash of white wine to the bottom of the tray.

6 Meanwhile prepare the ingredients for the peas.

7 You will know when your chicken is cooked because you can pull a leg away from the carcass with real ease. The juices must run clear. When cooked, remove the bird from the oven and leave to rest for at least 10 minutes.

8 Add the lardons to a large dry frying pan and cook until they start to turn golden and crispy. At this stage add the garlic, cook for a few minutes then throw in the peas. Add the chicken stock and allow to boil for a few minutes to reduce a little.

9 Add in the shredded lettuce, sugar and the seasoning. Remember to taste as you go. At this stage you can pour in any juices that are now on the resting plate from the chicken.

10 At the last minute, add a squeeze of lemon juice, the mint and stir in the butter and flour mixture. This will thicken the sauce slightly and give you a gravy.

11 When the sauce cooks a little, carve your chicken into thick slices or leave the breasts whole, skin on, if you prefer. Spoon a ladleful of the pea mixture into serving bowls and lay the chicken on top. Perfect teatime dinner.

pan-fried mackerel
with fennel, grapefruit, caper & parsley salad

This is a great light supper for when you're in a rush or just don't want a lot of fuss. The only cooking involved is the mackerel, and that only takes about 5 minutes. Plus it looks great; after all, they do say we eat with our eyes. A perfect example of simplicity at its best. I've used caperberries which have a mellower flavour than pickled capers, but use whichever you prefer. If you buy salted capers, rinse them in cold water first, otherwise they will be far too salty for this dish.

SERVES 2

FOR THE SALAD
4 fillets fresh mackerel
1 large bulb of fennel
1 lemon

1 pink grapefruit
A handful of caperberries
A bunch of flat leaf parsley
A handful of watercress (optional)
1 tablespoon olive oil, plus extra for drizzling
Salt and freshly ground black pepper

1 When you buy the mackerel, ask your fishmonger to remove the bones down the middle of the fillets. This is done by cutting a v-shape on either side of the bones and removing them all in one go. If you're brave, try it yourself.

2 To make the salad, cut the fennel in half and remove the core by cutting a v-shape on either side and easing it out. (You can eat this but it is a bit tough and can be bitter.) Slice the fennel by turning it flat side down and slicing very thinly downwards. Squeeze half the lemon over the fennel to prevent it from going brown.

3 Peel the skin from the grapefruit using a sharp, serrated knife, trying to remove all the pith with the skin as you do this. Using your knife, remove each segment of fruit and add it to a large bowl. Squeeze in any juice from the bits you have cut off.

4 Add the fennel to the grapefruit along with the caperberries. Pick off the leaves from the flatleaf parsley and throw them into the bowl, with the watercress, if using; I find this adds a lovely peppery element.

5 To cook the mackerel, heat the oil in a large non-stick pan. Season the skin-side of the fillets with salt (Maldon sea salt is best), and place in the pan, skin-side down. Hold them flat in the pan with a fish slice to prevent them curling. Cook on each side for 2 minutes.

6 Add a final squeeze of lemon and remove from the heat. Place a nice big pile of the salad onto a plate and top with the fish. Sprinkle with salt, pepper and a good drizzle of olive oil. Delicious.

TIP This recipe is good for all oily fish as the acidity from the grapefruit really cuts through the richness.

tequila chicken wings

The best snack for when you have a full house. If your friends are anything like mine, anything that contains booze is always a hit.

SERVES 6–8

FOR THE PASTE
Zest and juice of 4 limes
3 tablespoons sugar
2 red chillies, deseeded or not, depending on how
    brave you are
2 garlic cloves
1 teaspoon salt

75ml tequila
1 tablespoon runny honey
1 tablespoon vegetable oil
1.5kg chicken wings
Lime wedges, to serve

1 Pound together all the ingredients for the paste using a pestle and mortar.

2 When it is quite fine, add the tequila and honey and mix well. Add the oil (this stops the paste from burning) and massage into the wings.

3 Leave to marinate in a non-metallic dish for as long as you can; overnight is great.

4 Preheat the oven to 180°C/350°F/Gas Mark 4. Cook the chicken wings for 20 minutes. Serve with lime wedges and shots of tequila.

pork chops on the bone

with 'all the right stuff'

People are often put off by pork chops because they think the meat is going to be dry and tough. This is truly not the case (well, not when cooked correctly at least). Pork can be eaten slightly 'blushed'; it doesn't need to be grey to be safe to eat. OK, it can't be eaten as you would eat a rare steak, but a little rosiness is fine and means the moisture is still in the meat, making it tender and succulent.

SERVES 4

2 eating apples, peeled, cored and cut into eighths
2 garlic cloves, peeled and sliced in half
4 thick pork chops on the bone with a good layer of fat rind
2 sprigs of thyme, leaves removed

Zest of 1 lemon, plus a squeeze of the juice
2 tablespoons olive oil
50g butter
150ml cider
2 tablespoons wholegrain mustard
100ml double cream

1 Preheat the oven to 180°C/350°F/Gas Mark 4.

2 Lay the apple quarters on a roasting tray. Rub the garlic over the pork chops and season with the thyme leaves, the zest of the lemon and the olive oil.

3 Heat a griddle pan and place the seasoned chops on it just long enough to seal both sides and the fatty rind. When the griddle lines have appeared, put the chops on top of the apples and dot a small amount of butter on each one.

4 Pour the cider into the tray and cook in the oven for 12–14 minutes, depending on the thickness of the chops. They should feel firm to the touch.

5 Remove from the oven and leave the chops and the apples to rest on a warm plate while you make the sauce.

6 Place the empty roasting tray on the stove and turn up the heat. Scrape all the roasty toasty bits off the bottom of the tray and add the mustard, cream and a squeeze of lemon. Allow to reduce slightly.

7 Serve the chops with the roasted apples and the sauce. Great with a big bowl of creamy mash on the side.

sizzled mussels

When anyone thinks about cooking mussels, they always assume that the only way to do it is to 'sweat the garlic, add the mussels, pour in the wine and steam open'. Well, that's a great classic method, but how about something a bit different?

SERVES 2

1 red chilli, finely sliced
2.5cm knob of ginger, peeled and finely sliced
2 garlic cloves, finely sliced

1–1½kg mussels, cleaned, beards removed
100ml Noilly Prat (or other white vermouth)
½ bunch of coriander, chopped
25g butter
1 lime, for squeezing

1 Ensure your chilli, ginger and garlic are prepared and your mussels thoroughly cleaned and checked; any with broken or open shells should be discarded.

2 Heat up a large griddle pan until it's really, really hot. Throw in the mussels along with the chill, ginger and garlic.

3 When the mussels start to sizzle and the liquid starts to come out, pour in the Noilly Prat, cover the pan, and allow the mussels to steam open (check after 4 minutes).

4 Throw in the coriander at the last minute and fold through the butter. Serve with a good squeeze of lime.

hot tea-smoked salmon

with soy and honey glaze

Hot smoking is a fantastic way to inject flavour into meat and fish. You don't need a fancy smoker if you have a wok and a trivet and it's a very quick and cheap process.

SERVES 4

FOR THE SMOKING
100g rice
100g brown sugar
50g black tea leaves
1 star anise
2 cardamon pods

FOR THE MARINADE
1 tablespoon soy sauce
1 tablespoon honey
1 tablespoon olive oil

4 x 150g fillets organic salmon, skin off
Salt
2 teaspoons sesame seeds, toasted

1 To make your wok into a smoker, line it with a double layer of tin foil. Pour in the rice, sugar, tea leaves, star anise and cardamon pods. Mix thoroughly. Place a trivet in the wok so that the salmon is not in direct contact with the rice and tea mixture. (If you have a bamboo steamer, you can place it on top of the trivet, if not, simply lay a sheet of baking parchment on the trivet and cook directly on that.)

2 To make the marinade for the salmon, simply mix all the ingredients together and brush it over the fish. Season with salt.

3 Put the wok on a low heat and cover with a lid or tin foil to prevent the smoke from escaping. When you start to smell the smoke, place the salmon fillets on the trivet or in the steamer. Cover with the lid or foil and cook for 5–6 minutes. Depending on how thick your salmon is, you may need to finish cooking it in the oven, preheated to 170°C/325°F/Gas Mark 3 for 4–5 minutes at the most. Don't leave the fish in the smoker for longer than 6 minutes as it may start to turn bitter.

4 When the fish is cooked, remove from the pan, brush with the remaining glaze, sprinkle with the sesame seeds and serve. This is great with simple steamed rice and a cucumber salad.

TIP Steaming over rice and tea works really well with any oily fish robust enough to cope with the flavours. Don't use a delicate fish. This method is also great if you want to infuse the smoky flavour into meat.

 TIP Do not leave your risotto alone on the heat. It needs constant love and attention.

retro risotto

beetroot and goat's cheese

This is probably the most outrageously coloured plate of food you will ever cook.

SERVES 4

2 large beetroot
50g butter
2 shallots, finely chopped
1 leek, white part only, finely chopped
1 garlic clove, chopped
Sprig of thyme, leaves only
350g arborio rice

150ml white wine
1 litre hot vegetable stock, ideally homemade but
    from a cube is okay
150g goat's cheese, crumbled
75g Parmesan, finely grated

1 Peel and dice the beetroot as small as you can.

2 Melt the butter in a shallow-sided pan and add the shallot, leek, garlic and diced beetroot. Cook them slowly and allow the vegetable to go translucent. Once this has happened, add the thyme and rice. Turn the rice over in the now purple ingredients and ensure that every grain is coated in the butter.

3 Turn up the heat slightly and add the white wine. Keep the rice moving at all times. When the liquid has all been absorbed, add a ladleful of hot stock. Continue to add a ladleful at a time, stirring to keep the rice constantly on the move. This takes about 15 minutes.

4 When the rice is just under done, add the goat's cheese and the Parmesan. Correct the seasoning with salt, if necessary, and serve.

velvet chocolate crème brûlée

This takes very little effort to prepare, but keep in mind that it's often best to let them chill overnight.

SERVES 4–5

500ml double cream
1 vanilla pod, split

6 egg yolks
120g caster sugar
100g good-quality plain chocolate

1 Preheat the oven to 170°C/325°F/Gas Mark 3.

2 Gently heat the cream in a saucepan with the vanilla.

3 Whisk together the egg yolks and the sugar. Break the chocolate into small pieces and add to the egg mixture.

4 When the cream comes to the boil, pour it over the egg and chocolate mix, whisking all the time so the eggs don't scramble. Pass through a fine sieve into a clean jug.

5 Pour the mixture into 4 or 5 ovenproof ramekins and place in a baking tray. Fill the tray halfway up the ramekins with boiling water, put in the oven for 15–20 minutes. All ovens vary so if it takes longer than this, don't worry. You will know when they're ready because they will be set on top with a slight wobble. Remove from the oven, allow to cool and then chill.

6 When you're ready to serve, sprinkle the tops with a light layer of caster sugar and caramelise using a cook's blowtorch or under a very hot grill. Leave the sugar to set for a few minutes before serving.

passionfruit set yogurt & mango sauce

SERVES 4

3 gelatin leaves
175ml double cream
2 large passionfruits, pulps and seeds
4 tablespoons runny honey
Zest and juice of 1 lemon
100g sugar

300g Greek yogurt

FOR THE MANGO SAUCE
1 large ripe mango, peeled and diced
80g icing sugar
Juice of ½ lemon
5 mint leaves

1 Chill 4 small tumblers in the fridge and put the gelatin leaves in cold water to soak.

2 In a saucepan, bring the double cream to a boil. Add the passionfruit, honey, lemon and sugar. Stir well, remove from the heat and cool for 10 minutes.

3 Squeeze out the gelatin and add to the mixture. Add the Greek yogurt and give it all a good whisk. Pour into the chilled glasses. Leave to set in the fridge for about 40 minutes.

4 Make the sauce by dropping the mango dice into a mini blitzer with the icing sugar, lemon and mint. Blitz until smooth. Pour a tablespoon of the mango sauce over each of the set yogurts and serve.

TIP The chocolate crème brûlée would also look great served in espresso cups, in which case this is enough for 8 servings.

127

show-off suppers

This is my cheffy side... simplified. I hope this chapter inspires you to phone friends and tell them to expect a treat. These recipes are a step further than the previous ones, but are definitely possible for any occasional chef. I've purposely used ingredients that are a little more luxurious and perhaps a bit more expensive. Treat yourself and your friends.

smoked mackerel pâté

with caper & cornichon dressing

This is such an easy starter to make for a dinner party. It's best to make it during the day, so that you aren't spending the evening in the kitchen while your guests are enjoying themselves without you, and because the flavours of the pâté and dressing have time to mature. All you need is some nice soda bread to serve with it and a little salad. For best results, use a food-processor.

SERVES 6

FOR THE PÂTÉ

4 smoked mackerel fillets, skin removed
   (check for bones!)
150g cream cheese
10g crème fraîche
Juice of 1 lemon
½ teaspoon cayenne pepper

Salt and freshly ground black pepper

FOR THE DRESSING

50g pickled capers, rinsed and chopped roughly
50g cornichons (baby gherkins), chopped roughly
1 tablespoon Dijon mustard
1 teaspoon white-wine vinegar
Juice of ½ lemon
50ml olive oil

1 To make the pâté, place all the ingredients in a food-processor and whizz until smooth. Scrape the edges halfway through to incorporate all the bits. Taste for seasoning and to ensure there is enough lemon.

2 Spoon into 6 little pots or 125ml ramekins, smooth down the tops and place in the fridge.

3 To make the dressing, roughly chop the capers and cornichons and place in a small bowl. Spoon in the mustard, vinegar and lemon juice. Mix together then add the olive oil. Season lightly because the capers will already be quite salty.

4 Serve with slices of soda bread and perhaps a watercress salad drizzled with the dressing.

TIP Herbs can freshen and brighten a dish in seconds. Pick up a bag of dill or chervil to garnish this tasty little starter.

sage, pumpkin & parmesan gnocchi

Sometimes it can be hard to find a recipe to suit everyone if you are cooking dinner for a vegetarian, especially if the other guests are meat-eaters and expect something more substantial than a slice of nut loaf. This recipe will do the trick.

SERVES 6

1kg unpeeled floury potatoes, the larger the better
2 large or 3 small egg yolks
Salt and freshly ground black pepper
A few gratings of nutmeg
100g Parmesan, grated
225–250g plain flour, plus extra for dusting and rolling
50g butter
1 tablespoon olive oil

1 small pumpkin, peeled, seeds and fibres removed, and cut into 1cm dice
1 garlic clove, sliced
12 sage leaves, kept whole

TO SERVE
Extra-virgin olive oil
A large handful of pumpkin seeds
Shavings of Parmesan

1 Put the potatoes in a saucepan and cover with cold salted water. Bring to the boil and cook for about 30 minutes until tender but before they have absorbed too much water and started to disintegrate. Drain and leave to cool for a few minutes, but you need to peel them while still warm. I find the easiest way is to wear rubber gloves.

2 Mash the potatoes with a masher or, better still, pass through a potato ricer, one at a time. Add the egg yolks, salt, pepper, nutmeg and Parmesan cheese and work all the ingredients together. Gradually add the flour, enough for the mixture to feel no longer wet; it should be sticky and hold together nicely.

3 Turn out the mixture onto a floured surface and roll into sausage shapes 1cm thick. Then cut the 'sausage' into 1.5cm pieces and press each one with the back of a fork to make the characteristic indent in the gnocchi.

4 Put them into the fridge to firm up slightly.

5 Twenty minutes before you are ready to serve, put a large pan of salted water on the hob to boil and put the butter and oil in a large frying pan to melt. Add the diced pumpkin to the frying pan, turn the heat down low and allow to gently cook. Give it a little toss every couple of minutes and watch that it doesn't catch on the bottom.

6 After about 10–12 minutes, when the pumpkin has started to soften, add the sliced garlic and the sage. Season well with black pepper and check for salt.

7 Put your gnocchi, a few at a time, into the pan of boiling salted water. Don't overcrowd the pan. The second they start to rise to the surface they are cooked. Remove from the water with a slotted spoon and add the cooked gnocchi to the pumpkin and sage. Continue until all the gnocchi are cooked.

8 Serve in large pasta bowls, drizzle with extra-virgin olive oil, pumpkin seeds and Parmesan shavings.

seared scallops

with a julienne of gently sautéed vegetables & ginger dressing

Fresh, simply cooked scallops are an absolute delight. They are expensive and with good reason: the average scallop is 4–7 years old and has put up a big fight to avoid being caught. 'Julienne' is simply a posh way of saying your veg are cut the length and thickness of matchsticks or thinner if you can!

SERVES 4

FOR THE JULIENNE OF VEGETABLES
2 carrots (choose large ones to make your life easier)
2 courgettes
1 leek, white only

FOR THE GINGER DRESSING
5cm knob ginger, peeled and sliced into thin julienne
1 tablespoon syrup from a jar of stem ginger
Juice of 1 lemon

2 tablespoons caster sugar
1 teaspoon white-wine vinegar
2 tablespoons Noilly Prat (or white vermouth)

12 scallops, preferably diver-caught
Salt and freshly ground black pepper
100g butter
1 tablespoon water
1 tablespoon oil

Sprigs of chervil or pea shoots, optional garnish

1 First make the julienne of vegetables. Top, tail and peel the carrots. Using a swivel-head peeler, create thick ribbons. Do the same with the courgettes, but stop when you get to the seeds. Keep separate. Lay the ribbons on top of each other and cut them in half. Now cut the ribbons lengthways into 1mm thick slices. Take your time – you should end up with a spaghetti-like mass of veg.

2 Remove the outer layers from the leek and discard. Trim off the top leaving you with the white part only. Halve the leek lengthways and give it a good wash. Now remove the root, separate the leek into 3 or 4 layers at a time and cut in the same way you did with the carrots and courgettes.

3 Blanch the carrot sticks in boiling water for about 2 minutes and then refresh in cold water and drain. Do the same with the leeks but not the courgettes.

4 Make the ginger dressing. Simmer all the ingredients in a pan for about a minute, until the sugar dissolves. You won't have much but it's a light dressing, not a sauce.

5 Place the drained carrots, leeks and uncooked courgettes in a pan with half the butter and the tablespoon of water. Allow to wilt and heat through. Season well and pour over 1 teaspoon of the olive oil.

6 Heat a non-stick pan with the rest of the oil and season the scallops. Lay them in the pan, flat-side down. Cook for 30 seconds, turn over once golden, add the rest of the butter and cook for a further 30 seconds.

7 Remove from the pan. Using a folk, twist the 'spaghetti' of veg around, making a ball. Place on a plate, lay the scallops on top and spoon over a little of the ginger dressing. Garnish with chervil or pea shoots.

pan-fried quail with caramelised fig

This makes a perfect starter if you feel like really showing off without being too adventurous in the kitchen. Quail is a beautiful meat, not at all strong or gamey, rather, more sweet and extremely tender.

SERVES 4

4 quail, broken down into 2 breasts and 2 legs
Salt and freshly ground black pepper
50g butter

1 teaspoon oil
4 figs, two cut in half and two finely chopped
100ml balsamic vinegar
2 tablespoons brown sugar
Sprig of chervil, to garnish (optional)

1 To break down the quail yourself, first hold out the wings on a chopping board and use the heel of a knife or sharp scissors to remove each one. Run a sharp knife down the backbone from the neck. Starting on one side of the backbone, remove each breast by simply gliding the knife down the carcass and peeling the breast back as you go. Do the same on the other breast. Then make a cut in the inner legs of the bird, hold the legs flat on the board and either remove with one hit with the heel of the knife or cut through with scissors.

2 Season the quail breasts and the legs on all sides. Heat a non-stick pan with the butter and a drop of oil. Put in the quail legs first – being on the bone, these will take slightly longer than the breast. Cook for 2 minutes then add the breasts, skin-side down, and the fig halves, cut-side down, and allow everything to turn a golden-brown colour. Keep

basting the meat and the figs with the butter to ensure the meat stays moist and that the figs have plenty of flavour. Add a tiny bit more butter if necessary. Turn over the quail and the fig after the legs have cooked for 4 minutes and the breasts for 2 minutes. After about 5 minutes, the quail will be ready.

3 Remove the quail and the figs from the pan and leave to rest in a warm place. Turn up the heat under the pan, add the balsamic, chopped figs and the brown sugar, and allow to reduce by half.

4 Arrange the quail in a neat stack on serving plates. Serve one fig half on each portion, presentation side (flesh side) out, and drizzle with some of the fig balsamic. Garnish with a sprig of chervil.

TIP This dish needs to be cooked just before you intend to serve it. It won't hold. However the preparation of the birds can be done way in advance, along with the tiny bit required for the fruit.

herb-crust rack of lamb

Rack of lamb is one of the easiest roasted joints you can prepare because it takes such little time to cook. Your usual 8-bone rack of French-trimmed lamb will take 15–18 minutes in the oven. Ask your butcher to prepare the French-trimmed racks of lamb, fat removed, don't attempt this yourself.

SERVES 5

FOR THE CRUST
Zest of 2 lemons
50g dried breadcrumbs
2 garlic cloves, crushed
A bunch of parsley, finely chopped
2 anchovy fillets
Leaves from 2 sprigs of thyme

2 bulbs of garlic
Olive oil, for drizzling
Salt and freshly ground black pepper
2 x 8-bone racks of French-trimmed lamb
Dijon mustard

FOR THE JUS
1 tablespoon flour
1 glass of white wine
1 tablespoon redcurrant jelly
2 sprigs of thyme
100ml chicken stock (made with a cube is okay)

1 For the crust, place all of the ingredients in a food-processor and blitz until fine. Leave to one side. The crust will keep well for a few days so go ahead and do it in advance if you can.

2 Preheat the oven to 180°C/350°F/Gas Mark 4.

3 Squash the garlic bulbs to separate the cloves but leave them intact with their skins on. Scatter into a roasting tin, drizzle with olive oil. Generously season the lamb and then place on top of the garlic, so the bones are slotting in towards each other making a trestle. Transfer to the oven for 5 minutes (set a timer). When the 5 minutes is up, remove the lamb and lightly brush with mustard (this is to make the crust stick). Lower the temperature to 160°C/325°F/Gas Mark 3.

4 Press the herb crust evenly on the lamb and return

it the oven for 10–12 minutes. The meat should feel firm but still have 'give' when cooked to medium-rare. Remove the lamb from the tray along with most of the garlic. Leave to rest in a warm place for as long as possible – this is essential.

5 To make the jus, place the roasting tin on the hob. Add the flour to soak up the juices. When it is really hot, deglaze with the wine and scrape off all the bits from the base of the tin. If it starts to go lumpy, change to a whisk to remove the lumps. Add the redcurrant jelly, the thyme and the chicken stock. Allow to simmer and cook for 3–4 minutes then strain through a sieve.

6 Carve the meat, 3 chops per person with 1 chop left over for the cook! There have to be some perks when cooking! Serve with the roasted garlic and the jus.

crispy pork belly

with black pudding mash & caramelised apples

Pork belly is always something I really fancy in a restaurant but it often disappoints. It's one of those dishes that needs to be cooked and eaten straight away. However with this recipe, you can do most of the work during the day, even the day before, then finish it off just before you are ready to serve. It's great with all things porky: cider, apples, fennel… but my favourite is with black pudding mash.

SERVES 6–8

1 bulb of fennel, sliced thickly
1 bulb of garlic
½ belly of pork, ribs removed
Maldon sea salt
1 tablespoon fennel seeds
1 litre olive oil

FOR THE BLACK PUDDING MASH
1.5kg peeled floury potatoes
100ml double cream
80g butter
Salt
300g black pudding, skin removed and diced into
    small chunks

FOR THE SAUCE
1 shallot, diced
2 peppercorns
1 sprig of thyme
1 bay leaf
500ml cider
1 tablespoon liquid beef concentrated stock
300ml double cream

FOR THE CARAMELISED APPLES
1 teaspoon vegetable oil
50g butter
2 eating apples, peeled, quartered and cored
2 tablespoons brown sugar

1 Preheat the oven to 150°C/300°F/Gas Mark 2.

2 Place the fennel on the bottom of a 5cm deep roasting tray. Put the garlic in the tray.

3 Score the pork belly with a really sharp knife in a criss-cross fashion. Season it all over with the Maldon salt and the fennel seeds. Rub into the flesh and the scored skin. Place the pork on the fennel 'trivet', skin-side up. Pour in the olive oil so it covers the pork halfway up the sides. Cover with foil and transfer to the oven. Cook for at least 3 hours until the pork is really tender.

4 Remove the pork belly from the oil and place on a metal trivet over another tray. Increase the oven temperature to 220°C/425°F/Gas Mark 7. If you want, you can portion it at this stage.

5 Season the skin again generously with Maldon salt and cook until the skin is golden brown, crispy and puffed up. This will take about 25–30 minutes; you may need to turn the tray round halfway through to ensure even cooking of the crackling. Remove from the oven, cut into squares with a serrated knife and serve.

6 Meanwhile, prepare the accompanying dishes. For the black pudding mash, peel the potatoes and cut in half, no smaller otherwise they will take on too much water while cooking. Place in cold water with plenty of salt and slowly cook until they are soft and almost falling apart. Drain them well and place back on the hob to dry them out. This will give you a firmer mash.

7 Now, using a potato ricer, pass the potatoes through, one by one. You can use a masher, but it won't be nearly as smooth. At this stage you can store the mash if working ahead, or you can finish it now. Heat the cream and butter and slowly pour it into the mashed potatoes bit by bit, stirring all the time. Beat well and season with plenty of salt. Add the black pudding. Return to a low heat to beat in the pudding and to heat the mash and the pudding through. Keep warm until ready to serve.

8 To make the sauce, heat the shallot, peppercorns, thyme, and bay leaf in a pan with the cider to reduce by half. Add the stock concentrate and the cream. Reduce again until the sauce is thick enough to coat the back of a spoon. (You won't have much but this is a seasoning, not a gravy.) Strain and keep warm until needed.

9 Finally, for the apples, heat the oil in a non-stick frying pan and add the butter. When it starts to bubble slightly, add the apples and the sugar. You may need to work in batches, cooking 4–6 quarters at a time. Allow them to develop a golden-brown colour, but don't let them burn or overcook. Try not to move the pan too much or the apple quarters will break up.

10 To serve, spoon the mash onto serving plates. Place the pork belly on top, finish with the apples and a drizzle of the sauce.

TIP Although this may seem time-consuming to prepare, everything can be done in advance – just crisp the belly before you are ready to serve.

 TIP The duck fat can be used again and again. Of course the more times you use it the better the flavour. You can use it each time you want to make a confit, not just for duck.

confit of duck leg

with cassoulet of beans

Confit is just a posh word meaning 'slow cooked in fat'. It tastes great because the method allows all the flavours to infuse slowly. Cassoulet is the name of a classic French dish made from duck, sausage, pork belly and beans. My version is simplified from the traditional 3-day method.

SERVES 4

FOR THE CONFIT

4 duck legs, preferably large ones with plenty of fat on them

200g salt (for the cure – you wont eat this!)

2 bay leaves

Zest of 1 orange, removed with a speed peeler or knife

5 black peppercorns

1 bulb of garlic, cut in half horizontally

2 sprigs of thyme

500ml duck fat (sold solidified in tins and jars)

FOR THE CASSOULET

200g smoked pancetta, cut into lardons

1 tablespoon duck fat

2 garlic cloves, sliced

1 red onion, finely sliced

1 carrot, finely diced

1 leek, white part only, finely diced

1 bay leaf

200ml red wine

1 teaspoon tomato purée

400g tinned borlotti beans, drained

400g tinned canellini beans, drained

200ml beef stock

Leaves from a sprig of thyme

Salt and freshly ground black pepper

1 Firstly, cure the duck legs overnight. Place the duck in a bowl, pour over all the salt and massage into the legs. Cover and leave overnight in the fridge. The following day, remove the duck from the fridge and wash off all the salt in cold water.

2 Preheat the oven to 150°C/300°F/Gas Mark 2. Place the legs in a baking dish. Add in all the flavouring ingredients. Melt down the duck fat in a pan and pour it over the duck. Cover with tin foil or a lid and place in the oven. Check often to ensure the fat isn't bubbling. If it is, reduce the temperature slightly. Cook for about 1½ hours.

3 Next, make the cassoulet. First, fry off the pancetta lardons in the duck fat. When they turn golden brown, reduce the heat and add the garlic, onion, carrot, leek and bay leaf. These should be cooked slowly, without allowing them to colour. When they start to soften, add the wine and reduce by half before adding the tomato purée. Stir until it has all been incorporated and the juices start to thicken. Stir in the beans, then add the beef stock. Simmer slowly for 15 minutes, and allow the beef stock to reduce. Finally add the thyme leaves. Season with salt and pepper.

4 You will know when the duck legs are cooked because the meat will nearly be falling of the bone. Remove from the fat and take the skin off the legs. This should come off easily. Reheat the skinless duck legs in the cassoulet and serve.

beef wellington

I have decided to bend a few rules with the classic wellington recipe. The method is basically the same, but I've changed some of the ingredients you would usually find in a Wellington. Fillet of beef is expensive but it's okay to spoil yourself once in a while. Ask for centre cut to ensure even cooking.

SERVES 2

50g butter
4 shallots, diced
2 garlic cloves, crushed
6 Portobello mushrooms, peeled and diced
Sea salt and freshly ground black pepper

300g spinach
1 tablespoon olive oil
500g piece of beef fillet (ask for the centre cut)
500g ready-made puff pastry
Flour, for dusting
1 egg, combined with 20ml milk to make an eggwash

1 Preheat the oven to 180°C/350°F/Gas Mark 4.

2 Melt the butter in a frying pan and add the shallots and garlic. Cook for about 5–6 minutes or until the shallots have turned transparent. Add in the mushrooms and cook down a little more before pouring the mix into a sieve to drain off the excess liquid. Allow to cool for 15 minutes in the fridge.

3 Briefly cook the spinach in boiling salted water until wilted. Drain and refresh in cold water. Press between two plates to remove excess water and set aside.

4 The next job is to seal the meat. Heat the frying pan with the oil. Season the meat well, and lay in the hot oil for just a few seconds on all sides until the meat has a bit of colour and is sealed. This will also add flavour. Remove from the pan and set aside.

5 Roll out the pastry on a floured surface to make a rectangle about 2–3mm thick. Lay the spinach on the pastry, leaving a 2cm gap on three sides and at least 4cm on the fourth side. Evenly spread the mushroom mixture over the spinach.

6 Place the beef fillet on top of the spinach and mushrooms on the side nearest to you. Brush the edges with the eggwash and roll the wellington up tightly to completely cover the fillet. Trim off any excess pastry and seal the ends up by simply tucking them under the roll. (You can prepare the dish up to this point in advance.)

7 Put the parcel on a baking tray, brush the surface with eggwash and sprinkle with sea salt. Bake for 25 minutes. Remove from the oven and allow the Wellington to rest for at least 5 minutes before cutting it in half and serving.

rich langoustine lasagne

& chervil and gruyère cream sauce

SERVES 4

1 quantity Pasta Dough recipe (see page 150)
24 langoustines

FOR THE COURT BOUILLON
1 bulb of fennel, sliced
½ bottle dry white wine
200ml water
1 onion, sliced
2 peppercorns
1 star anise

FOR THE SAUCE
20g butter
2 shallots, finely chopped

½ garlic clove
1 leek, white part only, finely chopped
Sprig of thyme
Stalks from a bunch of chervil, leaves reserved
   as garnish
All the langoustine shells and 200ml of the court
   bouillon (see above)
2 teaspoons tomato purée
50ml Pernod
200ml double cream
50g gruyère cheese
Juice of ½ lemon
Pinch of cayenne pepper
1 egg yolk, at room temperature

1 Make the pasta according to the instructions on page 150.

2 Place the langoustines in a large pan and add all the court bouillon ingredients. Poach for 5–6 minutes then remove the langoustines. Allow to cool slightly then remove the heads, claws and outer shells (reserve the shells for flavouring the sauce). Set aside.

3 Melt the butter in a large pan and sweat the shallot, garlic, leek, thyme, chervil stalks and langoustine shells. When the veg starts to turn translucent, add the court bouillon, tomato purée and Pernod and allow to reduce. Add the double cream and again allow to reduce slowly for 20 minutes or so, on a low heat. Add the cheese. When it has slightly thickened, add a squeeze of lemon and the cayenne pepper. Strain through a sieve.

4 Remove the pasta from the fridge. Pass half through a pasta machine set to the second-last setting. Cut into 6cm squares and store between baking parchment while you roll out the other half in the same way. You may need to use a little flour to prevent it from sticking.

5 Assemble the dish. Prepare a pan of boiling water and cook the pasta for 3 minutes. Reheat the sauce gently, adding the langoustine meat at the last minute, along with the egg yolk. Spoon a small amount of the sauce into the base of a serving plate followed by a layer of pasta and a few langoustines. Repeat so that you have three layers, finishing with a covering of sauce. Glaze under a grill for a few minutes and garnish with a sprig or two of chervil. Wow that's a show-off dish!

melting chocolate fondants

I have never met anyone who didn't have a soft spot (if you'll allow me the pun) for these puddings. Cook and serve them immediately, otherwise the molten chocolate centre will continue to cook and you'll end up with sponge rather than fondant and no doubt some very disappointed guests.

The hardest bit is turning them out. Do it quickly; the chances of the pudding collapsing are far greater if you try to take your time. To make it easier, you need 6, preferably non-stick, ramekins. If you don't have any, ordinary mini pudding basins are fine as long as they are properly greased and dusted with cocoa powder.

SERVES 6

150g butter, plus extra for greasing the moulds
6 teaspoons cocoa powder, plus extra for decoration
150g good-quality chocolate (about 70% cocoa solids), broken into small pieces

3 whole eggs
3 egg yolks
180g caster sugar
150g plain flour
Clotted cream, to serve

1 Preheat the oven to 160°C/325°F/Gas Mark 3.

2 Grease each mould with butter and place a teaspoon of cocoa powder in each one. Turn them so the powder lines the sides and the base without gaps. This will prevent the fondant from sticking. Knock out any surplus cocoa. Place in the fridge until the mix is ready.

3 Melt the butter and the chocolate in a heatproof bowl over a saucepan of simmering water. When it has all melted, remove from the heat and leave to cool.

4 Whisk the eggs and egg yolks with the sugar until slightly pale and fluffy. Add the cooled chocolate mix and slowly stir in. Sift the flour into the mix and gently fold in.

5 Divide equally between the moulds and bake for 10 minutes. Remove from the oven and turn each out onto serving plates by placing the plate on top of the mould and, using a tea towel so not to burn yourself, tip the ramekin upside down. The pudding should slip out easily. If not, use a little knife to help release it. Dust with cocoa and serve with the clotted cream.

TIP You can keep these fondants uncooked in the fridge until needed. Increase the cooking time by 2 minutes as the mix will be cold.

poached pears

with honey mascarpone

This is possibly one of the easiest desserts to make and always a crowd pleaser. The pears don't have to be cooked for hours as you might think, especially if they're ripe.

SERVES 6

FOR THE POACHING LIQUOR
1 bottle red wine
200g caster sugar
Zest of 1 orange, removed with a swivel peeler
1 star anise
2 cloves
1 cinnamon stick
1 cardamom pod, squashed
2 black peppercorns

6 ripe pears
3 tablespoons runny honey
300g mascarpone

1 Place all the poaching ingredients in a pan and slowly bring to the boil.

2 Peel the pears and remove as much of the core as you can, using a teaspoon. This doesn't involve cutting the pear in any way, simply twisting the spoon in the base of the pear to remove the main bit of the core. Leave the stalks on for presentation.

3 When the poaching liquor starts to come to the boil, turn the heat to almost nothing and place the pears in the stock. Give them a turn halfway through to ensure they are taking up the colour and flavour on all sides. Poach for about 10 minutes; the pears shouldn't really need any cooking, unless they are underripe in which case poach them slowly until a knife easily pierces the flesh without resistance.

4 Remove the pan from the heat and allow the pears to cool down in the poaching liquor. Serve warm. To reheat, just return the pan to the hob with the pears in it and bring to the boil.

5 Mix the honey with the mascarpone and serve on the side. Make sure everyone gets a fair share of liquor and pear. If you want, you can also reduce the poaching liquor to a syrup and pour over.

lemon & raspberry tart

It's hard to beat a wonderfully indulgent lemon and raspberry tart. They look and taste fantastic – a sure-fire way to impress guests. This will make up to 12 portions, and will last if not eaten straight away (although, that's probably unlikely to happen!). A 22–25cm flan case with a removable base and 2cm sides is what you need, and a non-stick one is best.

MAKES 12 PORTIONS

1 x Sweet Pastry recipe (page 156)
Butter, for greasing
Flour, for rolling

FOR THE FILLING

155g caster sugar
6 small or 5 large egg yolks, preferably organic free-range
Zest of 4 lemons, juice of 1½ lemons
150ml double cream
200g raspberries

Icing sugar, for dusting

1 Put the sweet pastry in the fridge for 30 minute. To make the tart, grease the flan case with butter on the sides and on the base. Remove the sweet pastry from the fridge. Dust your work surface with plain flour to prevent the pastry from sticking and start to roll it out, turning the pastry every couple of rolls and dusting with extra flour if needed. Roll the pastry to about 2mm thick.

2 Place the rolling pin at the top end of the rolled-out pastry and roll it around the rolling pin, then move it over to the flan ring and gently lay it into the tin. Don't worry too much if it breaks, you can very easily patch it up with the leftover pastry. Gently press the pastry into the edges of the pastry case (this is important, otherwise it will shrink). Trim off the excess pastry using a knife and leave in the fridge to rest.

3 Meanwhile, preheat the oven to 180°C/350°F/Gas Mark 4 and make the filling. Whisk the sugar and egg yolks together until pale white. Use an electric whisk if you prefer. Add the lemon zest and juice.

4 Heat the cream in a small pan until it starts to boil. Remove it from the heat and slowly pour it over the egg and sugar mix, stirring all the time to prevent it from curdling. Allow to cool slightly.

5 Remove the pastry case from the fridge and place on a baking tray. Line the pastry with baking parchment, fill it with baking beans and bake blind for 10 minutes. Remove the beans and bake for a further 5 minutes or until the tart case has started to turn slightly golden brown.

6 Scatter the raspberries into the base of the tart case and then pour the lemon cream on top.

7 Reduce the oven temperature to 160°C/325°F/Gas Mark 3 and bake the tart for 35 minutes or until the filling is no longer wobbly when gently shaken. Remove from the oven and leave to cool for 1–2 hours. Dust with icing sugar and serve in slices. I like it with crème fraîche and fresh raspberries.

 Handle the pastry as little as possible to ensure a better end-product. Also, if you don't rest your pastry it will shrink as you cook it.

  TIP These will keep in the fridge for up to a week. However, you will need to re-roll them in cocoa as it will dissolve over time.

orange & rum chocolate truffles

If you really want to show off for some guests, here's how to do it. You can even go a step further and wrap these up in fancy little boxes and offer them as gifts. As with most desserts, best-quality chocolate is imperative.

MAKES 25–30

400ml double cream
30–50ml dark rum, according to your taste
Zest of 1 orange, grated on a microfine grater
400g dark chocolate (at least 70% cocoa solids), broken into pieces

FOR DUSTING, CHOOSE ANY OR ALL:
Nibbed almonds
Ground pistachios
Desiccated coconut
Cocoa powder

1 To make a chocolate ganache, gently bring the cream to the boil with the rum and the orange zest. Pour over the broken chocolate, slowly mixing all the time. When it has all melted, place in the fridge for 2–3 hours or until completely set.

2 Remove the chocolate ganache from the fridge. You will need to work in a cool place. Tip your chosen dustings onto separate plates.

3 Soak a teaspoon in a bowl of hot water and then use it to spoon out a spoonful of chocolate ganache. Drop it into your chosen dusting. Roll in the coating and place on baking parchment to set again in the fridge.

biscotti...
the posh italian biscuit

The biscotti you see at the end of a dinner party are usually shop-bought and served with the wrong accompaniment (coffee). They're supposed to be served with a sweet Italian wine.

MAKES 25–30

35g butter
2 teaspoons Marsala
3 whole eggs
2 yolks
300g sugar
425g flour, sifted
1 tablespoon baking powder
130g whole almonds
100g whole hazelnuts
A little butter or oil, for greasing

1 Preheat the oven to 180°C/350°F/Gas Mark 4.

2 Melt the butter in a small pan with the Marsala. In a bowl, whisk together the eggs, yolks and the sugar until you can see a tail in the mixture when you lift up the whisk. This is called ribbon stage and can easily be done with an electric whisk. Add the wine and butter mixture and fold in the flour and baking powder. Add the whole nuts and mix thoroughly.

3 Grease a tray with a little butter or oil and shape the wet dough into a cigar-like loaf. You probably have enough to make two. Don't put them too close together as they spread during cooking. Transfer the tray to the oven and bake for 40 minutes.

4 Remove and leave on the tray to cool before slicing. These biscotti will keep for 2 weeks in an airtight container.

basics

Even the pros swear by these recipes, which are essential to anyone's repertoire, whether you're a home cook or a Michelin-starred chef but you're not expected to know these off by heart. Here you have a few really useful recipes as well as the chance to learn some of the techniques and tips.

pasta dough

MAKES 500G. ENOUGH TO MAKE LASAGNE FOR 4 AND SPAGHETTI FOR 2–3

500g '00' flour
4 eggs and 6 egg yolks
1 teaspoon salt
1 tablespoon olive oil
2 tablespoons water with a pinch of saffron strands

1 Sieve the flour into a large mixing bowl and make a well in the centre. Crack in the eggs and yolks and work into the flour with your fingertips.

2 Add the salt and the olive oil. Gradually add the water (because you may not need it all) to make a soft dough. This can all be done in a food processor if you're feeling lazy.

3 Turn the dough out onto a surface and knead it as hard as you can until you have a smooth dough (no need to flour the surface unless you made the dough a bit too wet).

4 Wrap the dough with clingfilm and put in the fridge for at least 30 minutes before you use it.

pizza dough

MAKES ENOUGH FOR 2 THIN PIZZAS

7g dried yeast (1 level teaspoon)
1 teaspoon sugar
50ml warm milk mixed with 300ml warm water
650g strong plain flour
1½ tablespoons olive oil
2 teaspoons salt

1 Dissolve the yeast and the sugar in a third of the milk and water solution.

2 Sift the flour into a large mixing bowl and make a well in the centre. Pour a little of the dissolved yeast mixture into the well. Add the olive oil and start to combine it all using your fingertips. Start to add the rest of the liquid and the salt, but you may need a little more or a little less of the liquid – you need to judge when the mixture has come together and formed a firm dough.

3 Turn out the dough onto a lightly floured surface and knead for 5 minutes. Work the dough with the palms of your hands as this helps to develop the gluten in the flour.

4 Put the dough back in the bowl, cover with a tea towel and leave somewhere warm for 30 minutes or until the dough has doubled in size.

5 Remove the dough from the bowl and roll out with a little flour if need be until the dough is really thin.

basic vinaigrette

A vinaigrette should be made with the same technique as the mayo (see page 153) and the end product should be a similar consistency. However, the truth is that as long as you give it a good shake before you use it, the flavours will still be evenly distributed on whatever you're dressing.

MAKES ENOUGH TO DRESS 1 SALAD

Zest and juice of 1 lemon
1 tablespoon Dijon mustard
1 teaspoon honey
2 tablespoons white wine or sherry vinegar
Pinch of salt
150ml olive oil

1 Place the lemon zest and juice in a small bowl and mix in the mustard, honey, vinegar and salt. Whisk in the olive oil slowly until it's fully incorporated.

2 Decant into a jar or bottle and keep until needed (but don't put it in the fridge or the oil will become thick and cloudy). Shake well before using.

tomato sauce

A good basic tomato sauce is a great thing to keep in the fridge. When you next make some for pasta, a meat ragout or a pizza topping, just increase the quantities and put the rest in a jar. It will keep in the fridge for about a week and you'll be surprised by the number of dishes you can make with it.

SERVES 4 AS A SAUCE FOR PASTA

1 red onion, finely chopped
2 garlic cloves
1 teaspoon olive oil
Sprig of thyme
1 tablespoon tomato purée
½ glass of red wine
1 tablespoon balsamic vinegar
2 teaspoons sugar
400g tinned chopped tomatoes
Salt and freshly ground black pepper

1 Fry the onion and garlic in the oil until soft.

2 Stir in the thyme and the tomato purée then add the red wine. Cook to reduce by half then add the balsamic, sugar and the tinned tomatoes, reserving the tomato tin.

3 Half-fill the tin with water and add to the sauce.

4 Cook at a simmer for around 20 minutes. Season well with salt and pepper. Whizz the sauce and serve or allow to cool and store for up to a week in a jar in the fridge.

 TIP Vinaigrette doesn't just have to be for salad; it's great poured over cooked veg instead of butter, or over fish for added flavour.

hollandaise sauce

This is a really classic sauce that is truly unbeatable when the need to indulge is necessary. You can't cheat with it; it is what it is. Basically, butter enriched with egg yolk but gosh, it tastes great with a poached egg and smoked salmon. You can make the reduction in advance.

SERVES 4 PEOPLE

100ml white wine vinegar
1 shallot, sliced
4 black peppercorns
1 bay leaf

Zest and juice of ½ lemon
3 egg yolks
1 tablespoon water
175g butter, cubed
Salt

1 To make your reduction for the sauce, put the vinegar, shallot, peppercorns, bay leaf and lemon zest into a pan. Bring to the boil over a medium heat. Allow to reduce until there is virtually nothing left then pass it through a sieve.

2 Place a pan of water on the hob and bring to simmering point. Turn down the heat really low. Put the reduction into a bowl that sits on top of the pan without coming into contact with the simmering water. Whisk in the egg yolks and the tablespoon of water, keeping the pan over the heat.

3 Whisk in the butter one piece at a time and don't add more until the first lump has disappeared. Keep whisking all the time. If the bowl starts to get a bit hot, remove it from the pan of simmering water for a few seconds.

4 When the sauce is really thick, remove from the heat, season with salt and add lemon juice to taste.

5 You can keep this sauce. Cover for about an hour in a warmish place to prevent a skin forming.

VARIATION
For béarnaise sauce, just add tarragon to the reduction and then add chopped tarragon and chervil at the end. Great with a rare steak and homemade chips.

mayo *(...any flavour you fancy)*

Mayo is surprisingly easy to make; the hardest part is separating the eggs perfectly because you don't want any egg white in your mayo. If your mayo doesn't thicken, it might mean you've added the oil too quickly and it has split. If this happens, put another egg yolk in a different bowl and slowly add to the split mixture. Make sure the eggs are not cold when you do this.

MAKES 200ML, PLENTY FOR 2 TO DIP INTO

2 egg yolks (aim for no residual white)
1 teaspoon Dijon mustard
250ml vegetable or rapeseed oil

Juice of 1 lemon
½ teaspoon salt
Black pepper
Optional flavourings: grated garlic, chopped coriander, lime zest or a little finely chopped chilli

1 Place the perfectly separated yolks in a bowl and add the mustard. Give it a little whisk by hand to break the yolks. Now, drop by drop, add the oil. Make sure the first drop is incorporated into the yolks before you add the next one. The more you add, the thicker your mayo. Don't add too much oil at a time as this encourages the mayo to split. Be patient.

2 When it is the consistency you want, add the juice of the lemon to taste, salt and the pepper. Done! Flavour it by adding one of the optional flavourings.

stocks

These are the three stocks you're most likely to need. I haven't included beef stock because it's less used and, to be honest, beef bones are so much bigger than chicken that few people have a pan big enough to fit them.

Here's a list of the basic vegetables. Remember, there's no need to peel them; the skin is where all the flavour is. Cut each one into 5cm pieces.

Carrot (use less carrot than everything else or your
   stock will be too sweet)
Celery
Onion
Leek

BOUQUET GARNI (THE 'PERFUME' IN THE
STOCK), MADE FROM THE FOLLOWING:
Bay leaf, thyme, peppercorns, parsley stalks
and a bulb of garlic (split in half)

brown chicken stock

Brown stock is good for gravy with roast dinners and when making casseroles. This will make 5 litres worth of good chicken stock but don't worry if you don't have a 5-litre pan. If your pan is a bit smaller, you will end up with a more intensified stock (that's a good thing). The bones and veg shouldn't come more than halfway up the pan. If they do, reduce the quantities or divide the ingredients between two pans.

MAKES UP TO 5 LITRES

1kg vegetables (as listed above)
1.5kg chicken bones, skin or fat removed from
   the carcass

2 tablespoons tomato purée
½ bottle white wine
Bouquet Garni (as listed above)

1 Preheat the oven to 180°C/350°F/Gas Mark 4. Place all the veg on the bottom of a large roasting tray. Put the chicken bones on top and 'massage' the tomato purée into the bones.

2 Place the tray in the oven and roast until the bones are golden brown and the veg are slightly roasted. This should take about 30 minutes.

3 Transfer the contents of the tray to a big stockpot. Put the roasting tray on the hob on a low heat and pour in the white wine. Scrape any bits from the bottom of the tray and allow the liquid to reduce by half. Pour the reduced wine into the stockpot and top up the level to within 1cm from the top of the pan with cold water.

4 Add the bouquet garni, turn on the heat and bring to the boil. Remove any scum that forms with a ladle and discard. Now cover with a lid and cook on a low heat for 5–6 hours, topping up the water if the level gets too low.

5 When the stock is cooked, pass through a fine sieve into a clean bowl and leave to cool slightly before removing any fat that has collected on the surface using a spoon.

6 Cool completely and store as you wish, either in the freezer or in jars in the fridge. Stock will last for 3–4 days in the fridge.

white chicken stock

Great for soups, white sauces or just basic poaching. The quantities for a white chicken stock are exactly the same as for the brown stock but the method is slightly different.

MAKES UP TO 5 LITRES

1 Place all the Brown Chicken Stock ingredients (see opposite) except the tomato purée, which you don't need for this recipe, in your stock pot (there is no need to roast the bones first). Cover with cold water to within 1cm from the top of the pan, bring to the boil, remove any scum and leave to cook as before.

2 Pass the cooked stock through a fine sieve into a clean bowl and leave to cool slightly before removing any fat that has collected on the surface using a spoon.

3 Cool completely and store in the same way as the brown stock.

vegetable stock

Vegetable stock is extremely versatile and so easy to make. You can use it as a substitute for just about any stock. Half vegetables to water is the rule. Throw in a star anise if you have any.

MAKES UP TO 5 LITRES

1 Prepare the vegetables as above, cover with cold water and cook for about an hour. Leave the stock to get completely cold with the veg in it then strain and store in the same way as the brown stock (see opposite).

shortcrust pastry

MAKES ENOUGH FOR A 22–25CM TORT CASE OR 250G OF PASTRY

250g plain flour, sifted, plus extra for dusting
Pinch of salt
125g cold butter, cut into pieces
2–3 tablespoons cold water

1 Mix the flour and salt in a mixing bowl and add the butter pieces. Rub the flour and butter together using the tips of your fingers until it resembles breadcrumbs. Add the water little by little and start to bring the pastry together.

2 Knead into a ball, cover in clingfilm and put in the fridge for 30 minutes to rest.

sweet pastry

MAKES ENOUGH FOR A 25–30CM FLAN CASE

250g plain flour
70g ground almonds
150g cold unsalted butter, cubed
Zest of 1 lemon
100g icing sugar, sieved
1 egg yolk
about 30ml cold water

1 Sieve the flour into a large mixing bowl and add the ground almonds. Add the cold butter and rub together with your fingers until the mixture starts to resemble breadcrumbs, or, better still, put it in a food processor and blitz for 30 seconds.

2 Mix in the lemon zest and the icing sugar. Finally add the egg yolk and mix again with your fingers until all the pastry has come together. If it seems too dry, add in the cold water but don't overdo it.

3 When it is all kneaded together, wrap in clingfilm and chill for at least 20 minutes.

real custard

MAKES 500ML, ENOUGH FOR 5–6 PEOPLE

500ml double cream
1 vanilla pod or a few drops of vanilla extract
5 egg yolks
1 whole egg
100g caster sugar

1 Pour the cream into a saucepan and scrape the seeds from the vanilla pod using the tip of a pointed knife. Bring to a gentle boil (don't allow it to boil fast as it will burn on the bottom).

2 Meanwhile place the egg yolks and the whole egg in a bowl with the sugar and whisk together well. When the cream has boiled, slowly pour a small amount over the egg mix while whisking continuously; you end up with scrambled egg if you add it too fast. Pour over the rest of the cream, still whisking. When it is all incorporated, pour back into the pan and return to a low heat.

3 Using a plastic spatula, cook gently, stirring continuously, until the custard coats the back of a spoon. Once the sauce thickens, pass it through a sieve and serve.

finger-lickin' butterscotch

The sweetest and stickiest sauce you'll ever make. No one can resist it! Serve it with anything, even on your cornflakes if that's the type of thing you're into.

MAKES 500ML, ENOUGH FOR 5–6 PEOPLE

250g brown sugar
110g butter
250g golden syrup
275ml double cream
½ teaspoon vanilla extract

1 Place the sugar, butter and syrup in a heavy-based pan, and allow to melt on a low heat.

2 Give it a good stir and allow to come slowly to the boil. Cook for a couple of minutes. Ensure all the butter is stirred into the sugar and slowly add the cream (be careful if the cream is really cold because it might make the hot sugar spit) and the vanilla. Stir in well and cook for a further 1–2 minutes.

3 Serve hot or cold. The sauce keeps for ages in the fridge and can be re-heated in the microwave (say for 2 minutes on medium, depending on your microwave's capacity, then let it stand for 2 minutes).

really rich chocolate sauce

MAKES 250ML, ENOUGH FOR 3–4 PEOPLE

100ml double cream
30g caster sugar
100ml milk
200g dark chocolate (70% cocoa solids)
30g cold butter, cubed

1 Pour the cream, sugar and milk into a saucepan and bring to the boil.

2 Break the chocolate into small pieces and put in a bowl. Pour in the milk mixture and give it a good stir to melt the chocolate. Now whisk in the butter to give it a good shine.

3 Serve hot. This sauce keeps well in the fridge but will solidify – Just put it in a pan to re-melt gently. It's okay to reheat it in the microwave provided you place the jug or bowl, covered, in a bowl of warm water. Microwave on low power in 30-second bursts, stirring in between, until hot and melted.

conversion chart

WEIGHT (SOLIDS)	
7g	¼ oz
10g	½ oz
20g	¾ oz
25g	1oz
40g	1½ oz
50g	2oz
60g	2½ oz
75g	3oz
100g	3½ oz
110g	4oz (¼ lb)
125g	4½ oz
150g	5½ oz
175g	6oz
200g	7oz
225g	8oz (½ lb)
250g	9oz
275g	10oz
300g	10½ oz
310g	11oz
325g	11½ oz
350g	12oz (¾ lb)
375g	13oz
400g	14oz
425g	15oz
450g	1lb
500g (½ kg)	18oz
600g	1¼ lb
700g	1½ lb
750g	1lb 10oz
900g	2lb
1kg	2¼ lb
1.1kg	2½ lb
1.2kg	2lb 12oz
1.3kg	3lb
1.5kg	3lb 5oz
1.6kg	3½ lb
1.8kg	4lb
2kg	4lb 8oz
2.25kg	5lb
2.5kg	5lb 8oz
3kg	6lb 8oz

VOLUME (LIQUIDS)	
5ml	1 teaspoon
10ml	1 dessertspoon
15ml	1 tablespoon or ½ fl oz
30ml	1fl oz
40ml	1½ fl oz
50ml	2fl oz
60ml	2½ fl oz
75ml	3fl oz
100ml	3½ fl oz
125ml	4fl oz
150ml	5fl oz (¼ pint)
160ml	5½ fl oz
175ml	6fl oz
200ml	7fl oz
225ml	8fl oz
250ml (0.25 litre)	9fl oz
300ml	10fl oz (½ pint)
325ml	11fl oz
350ml	12fl oz
370ml	13fl oz
400ml	14fl oz
425ml	15fl oz (¾ pint)
450ml	16fl oz
500ml (0.5 litre)	18fl oz
550ml	19fl oz
600ml	20fl oz (1 pint)
700ml	1¼ pints
850ml	1½ pints
1 litre	1¾ pints
1.2 litres	2 pints
1.5 litres	2½ pints
1.8 litres	3 pints
2 litres	3½ pints

LENGTH	
5mm	¼ inch
1cm	½ inch
2cm	¾ inch
2.5cm	1 inch
3cm	1¼ inches
4cm	1½ inches
5cm	2 inches
7.5cm	3 inches
10cm	4 inches
15cm	6 inches
18cm	7 inches
20cm	8 inches
24cm	10 inches
28cm	11 inches
30cm	12 inches

acknowledgements

If someone had told me two years ago when I was a baby chef at Westminster Kingsway college that I was going to be the author of such a beautiful book, I think I would have laughed in their face. And, I think that my lecturers might have too. 'Ah, Mr Cottam, Stocker and Brown.' You're all wonderful, thanks for everything!

Cooking and writing about cooking are my favourite things in the whole world, but I never really thought that I could make a living from it. When I sat down to write my first recipe I thought I had a hard task ahead of me, especially since all that I'd ever written in the past generally acquainted to 'thank you' cards at Christmas, but the reality was that I couldn't type fast enough to keep up with the ideas running through my head.

I guess my inspiration first came from my beautiful Nanny Vera, who made the meanest meat pie in the world. I have memories of rolling pasty in the kitchen in Plaistow before I could even reach the work surface. And of course, my wonderful Mum, who is actually a better cook than me. But don't tell her I told you! Lemon meringue pie never tasted so good. And I can't forget Dad, although the only really good thing I can remember him cooking was a Shepherd's Pie. But it was a tasty Shepherd's Pie so I won't knock!

My point is that my favourite memories are always related to food. Sunday lunches at Kevin and Mandy's, where the red wine played just as big a part as the fabulous leg of roasted lamb.

One of the key people I relied on when writing this book was Anthony. Thank you for being so honest. You're a star, thanks so much!

I mustn't forget all the people who made this amazing experience happen. The wonderful, honest Robert Common, my agent, friend, business advisor and everything else that you could imagine. Thank you for all your time, help and commitment and for believing in me! You're one in a million.

Everyone at Kyle Cathie. The fabulous Danielle, I can't imagine anyone being better at their job than you are. Muna, for putting your trust in me. The unbelievably talented Kate Whitaker; a dream to work with and an absolute genius. And who can forget Lizzie, food stylist and friend? You're one in a million. If anyone needs to learn to multi-task, they should take a few lessons from you!

Again, to all my family and supporting friends (Hannah, Carly, Rosie and Katie), they would all kill me if I didn't mention their names at some stage. Love you all.

See Mum and Dad, the private education wasn't wasted! I love you both so much!

And Claire, I hope you have some wonderful times teaching Oliver to cook from this book.

I hope you all enjoy reading it as much as I enjoyed writing it.

index

MARKETING

Bern Wisner

CENTRAL OREGON COMMUNITY COLLEGE

Prentice Hall
Upper Saddle River, N.J. 07458

Library of Congress Cataloging-in-Publication Data

Wisner, Bern.
    Applied marketing / Bern Wisner.—1st ed.
      p. cm.
    Includes index.
    ISBN 0-13-368382-6
    1. Marketing.   I. Title.
  HF5415.W54894 1996
  658.8—dc20

95–3262
CIP

Acquisitions Editor: *Elizabeth Sugg*
Production Editor: *Tally Morgan*
Production Liaison: *Eileen M. O'Sullivan*
Director of Manufacturing & Production: *Bruce Johnson*
Manufacturing Manager: *Ed O'Dougherty*
Production Manager: *Mary Carnis*
Marketing Manager: *Frank Mortimer, Jr.*
Creative Director: *Marianne Frasco*
Designer: Sheree *Goodman*
Cover Designer: *Sheree Goodman*
Formatting/Page Makeup: *Carlisle Communications, Ltd.*
Printer/Binder: *Von Hoffman*

© 1996 by Prentice-Hall, Inc.
A Simon & Schuster Company
Upper Saddle River, New Jersey 07458

Printed in the United States of America

10 9 8 7 6 5 4 3 2 1

ISBN 0-13-368382-6

Prentice-Hall International (UK) Limited, *London*
Prentice-Hall of Australia Pty. Limited, *Sydney*
Prentice-Hall Canada Inc., *Toronto*
Prentice-Hall Hispanoamericana, S.A., *Mexico*
Prentice-Hall of India Private Limited, *New Delhi*
Prentice-Hall of Japan, Inc., *Tokyo*
Simon & Schuster Asia Pte. Ltd., *Singapore*
Editora Prentice-Hall do Brasil, Ltda., *Rio de Janeiro*